ADVANCED GOLF

Better shot-making
for better scoring –
every time you play

TO JENNY WISSON

and for Eric Eadie, Hector Uquhart,
Peggy Conley, Suzanne Strudwick and
all golfing friends and pupils around the world
for whom I hope the written word bridges
the distance between us

with thanks to Gary Smith for
participating in the photos and to photographers
Mark Newcombe, Peter Dazeley
and Keith Hayley

ADVANCED GOLF

GOLF

Better shot-making
for better scoring –
every time you play

VIVIEN SAUNDERS

STANLEY PAUL
LONDON

First published 1995

1 3 5 7 9 10 8 6 4 2

© Vivien Saunders

Vivien Saunders has asserted her right under
the Copyright, Designs and Patent Act, 1988 to
be identified as the author of this work

First published in the United Kingdom in 1995 by
Stanley Paul & Co Ltd
Random House, 20 Vauxhall Bridge Road,
London SW1V 2SA

Random House Australia (Pty) Limited
20 Alfred Street, Milsons Point, Sydney
New South Wales 2061, Australia

Random House New Zealand Limited
18 Poland Road, Glenfield,
Auckland 10, New Zealand

Random House South Africa (Pty) Limited
PO Box 337, Bergvlei, South Africa

Random House UK Limited Reg. No. 954009

A CIP catalogue record for this book
is available from the British Library

ISBN 0 09 173815 6

Design & make-up Graham Harmer/Roger Walker

Printed and bound in Great Britain by
Clays Ltd, St Ives plc

CONTENTS

INTRODUCTION

We have two routes to becoming better golfers. The first is to learn to do our best swing (with whatever shot) as often as possible – and preferably every time. The other route is to change our best swing. Do not confuse change with progress. Some, or in fact many, of the world's top golfers have swings which cosmetically may not be perfect; but they believe in them – and as near as damn it do them every time. They succeed through belief in their own individuality. Their aim at perfection is to make their best swing each time. It is probably true to say that the technically perfect often fall just below the handful of world beaters. Perhaps an over-emphasis on mechanics takes something away from the flair to win.

On the other hand, there are those at the top for whom some niggling technical weakness really is the clue to lapses in brilliance. In the short game, perfect technique is crucial – with far less difference between actions among the best.

There is not just one perfect swing; there are many. While some essentials are common to every ideal swing, there are other concepts which are at the very crux of one player's action and yet are the Achilles heel of another.

This book aims at taking the advanced golfer through the various swing concepts and short-game techniques which can improve his technical brilliance, his swing and clubface awareness and his ability to learn the essence of golf – the art of scoring.

THE HANDS, THE FEEL AND THE CLUBFACE

1

SHAKE HANDS AND MAKE FRIENDS

Golf is the only game in which it is continually necessary to review the way in which you hold your weapon. In most other sports, the weapon, whether it be a bat, stick or racquet, is in your hands the whole time. You make friends with it. The racquet, for example, becomes like a new large right hand. Whatever you do with your hand, you do with the racquet.

In golf, instead of having a new large hand to feel, you have a silly little hand on the end of a new long arm. And golfers don't always learn to make friends with the club – certainly not with every club in the bag. And that is the trick – to feel a friendly disposition towards every one. In golf, instead of having one weapon in the hand the whole time, we have to make friends with a whole set of clubs.

The first problem is in making a choice. Which club am I going to use? It produces indecision. One of the basic problems for many golfers is that almost every shot is hit with some doubt as to the choice of club. Indeed, some players only seem entirely sure and confident of their choice on the green with a putter! The rest of the time there is a niggling feeling that the tool chosen isn't up to the job.

Having chosen the club, it is crucial to be able to take hold of it and feel comfortable straight away. Newer golfers always feel rushed on the course and spend too little time with the grip. Experienced golfers don't always grip as well on the course as on the practice ground. Others, hitting shot after shot on the practice ground, develop a consistent grip but then fidget and fiddle on the course. Sometimes it is nerves, sometimes simply the reaction of trying to be comfortable with the club quickly.

The key to a good grip is to shake hands with the club and make friends with it. When meeting a new acquaintance and

The feeling of gripping a club well should be to shake hands with the club, pointing the fingers along the club and easing them back into position

shaking hands with him you point your fingers towards him – not your thumb. The same applies in the golf grip. The hand points predominantly along the club, fingers curling back to take hold of it, never extending the thumb down the shaft and forming a clumsy fist. To feel a good grip, have a colleague hold the club out towards you to grip. Go to shake hands with it with the left hand, fingers first. Form the grip. Follow with the right, again fingers first for a diagonal grip and elegant position.

But good golf is all about clubface feel. The face of the club must become your right hand and your right hand the clubface – with every club, that is, not just the odd favourite. With a good grip you should be aware of the clubface. You have to transmit feel from the tips of the fingers into the face and back again. Butter a slice of bread with a knife. It isn't as messy as using your fingertips! The knife becomes your fingertips. So must the face of the club become part of you. Do you feel it? Are you at one with it? Can you close your eyes and feel the way the clubface moves?

If only a modest racquet player, you can *feel* the racquet. If a modest golfer, you probably can't feel the clubface. Firstly, this is through having the club in your hand for less of the time than your racquet – familiarity. Secondly, you have up to 14 clubs to make friends with. Thirdly, the clubface sits off at an angle. It is as though, however lofted the club, you have

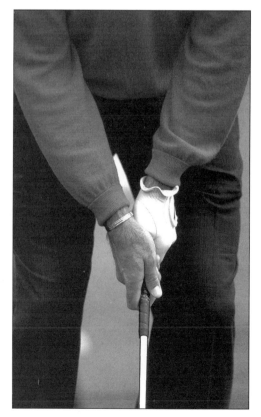

Seve's grip – right index finger triggered for power

to feel the clubface as though no loft exists. Some players line up the palm of the right hand and clubface with the driver, but then progressively let the right hand slide under as the lofts of the clubs increase.

To make friends with each and every club, grip each one with your eyes closed. Twiddle the club in your fingertips and regrip. It should come back naturally to a square position. The grip on a club is not round but egg-shaped, with the pointed part of the egg at the back of the grip. This should naturally steer you into gripping the club squarely and feeling the clubface. You might not want to butter a slice of bread with it, but the sensation shouldn't be far off!

For the aspiring champion, it is essential that your disposition towards every club in the bag is the same. Don't make the mistake of practising most with your best friend. Take the 2-iron, the 3-iron, the 3-wood and be able to hit the most delicate of shots with each. Learn to hit a soft fade or little punch with every club – including the driver – from 50 yards to its maximum, accurately to a target. Feel the spin in just the same way you would with a tennis racquet or with a sand wedge. In this way you learn to have no favourites. Your choice of club is more positive and objective.

Line up the right hand and the clubface. Take time to know each of the 14 friends who will accompany you through the joy (or pain) ahead!

CONSISTENCY

A good golfer is unlikely to get substantially the wrong grip. The most common faults usually involve fiddling and fidgeting under pressure or failing to unite the hands perfectly. The two tend to go together. If the hands aren't united satisfactorily, clubface feel is usually lost. A common fault among good golfers is letting the right hand sit too high on the left. Often this arises from a slightly strong left-hand grip, usually from starting as a junior, and then easing the right over too far. The hands aren't quite united with the left thumb properly in the palm of the right hand. This shows most easily from behind the player's shot, a gap showing between the second finger of the left hand and the right hand. The good golfer doesn't want the hands particularly extended but may for some reason try to unite the hands too closely.

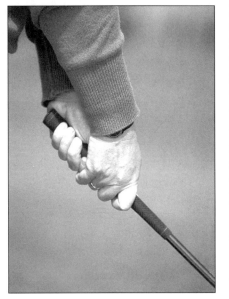

The correct view from behind a good grip

Wrong. In this grip the right hand has been brought too high up and too far over, the hands not quite uniting correctly

The feeling must be of being able to take any club from the bag and grip it easily and comfortably with the minimum of fiddling. Left hand, right hand and feel ready. If the slightest fidgeting emerges on the practice ground, it will be exaggerated under pressure. A good golfing method must allow for deterioration when tired or nervous. A fidgeting grip makes no such allowance. The grip clearly shouldn't change throughout the swing; some players' do. It isn't a question of gripping more tightly, but simply of remaining constant. Can you return from the end of one shot and be ready to hit another without any movement?

Ben Hogan, so I am told, hit over 20 2-woods, one after another, without having to regrip. Each, of course, landed on target. This may be a piece of golfing folklore, but I don't think so. The good golfer should be able to line up a row of 10 balls and fire them away without the slightest urge to hold too tightly, nor to regrip.

But fiddling before the club ever leaves address is often even more destructive. The player may start with a good grip and then, for example, squeeze a little harder with the right hand just before the takeaway. Or he may twitch and open and close the middle two fingers of the right hand. This may all seem very innocuous, but add a little pressure and the movement may be magnified.

As a rule, you don't stop a fidget. You have to replace it with something else. Fidgeters are usually saying 'Ready, steady, go', before launching themselves into action. Stop the movement and they may freeze. Instead, the mind needs to be focused on replacing the movement with another. A little kick in with the right knee is the surest. A forward press, even of minute proportions, is often too near the fiddling grip for comfort. Find another trigger movement to start the swing and a moving grip can be cured.

THE RULE OF THUMB

The grip of any professional golfer shows two definite spaces. The first is between the right index finger and the next. The right index finger is always triggered away slightly and never wrapped directly round the club. The curl of the index finger and that of the next finger are quite different. The index finger points far more along the club, the tip of the finger hardly in contact with the club. The professional could hit thousands of shots and never see any wear in the tip of the index finger. It is as though the finger points along the club and back towards you; never wrapped directly round the club. We talk of a 'trigger finger'. Hold the club out in front of you and imagine a gun with a trigger hanging beneath it. The right index finger is in a position to pull the trigger back towards you. In setting up to the ball, feel as though the index finger is about to shoot the ball!

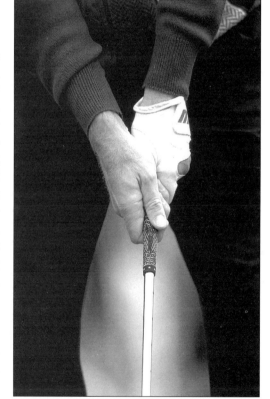

Nick Faldo– a typical one to two knuckle grip for the pro – a touch weak for most amateurs

This trigger position puts the power of the right index finger behind the club and aimed in the correct direction – at the target. The mistake club golfers often make is to pull the right index finger up and to wrap it directly round the club. Hand in hand with this goes a tendency to put the right thumb straight down the front of the club. It feels in control. But all the power of the thumb and index finger is now going in the wrong direction – not towards the target, but up and down. Great if you want to hit yourself on the head or knock in a tent peg!

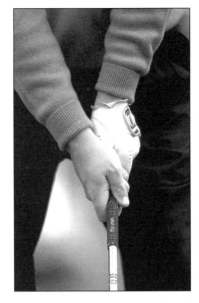

Ian Woosnam – a very sound grip to copy. Notice the position of the right thumb, never with any great golfer down the front of the club

Ray Floyd – here the right thumb is well round to the left; the further opened round to the left the more the likelihood of a draw or hook and the less of a slice

In the correct position, the right index finger is behind the club and the thumb slightly on the other side, with the inside of the thumb against the club. The two steady each other. Now the right index finger is in a powerful hitting position and can apply the leverage.

The precise position of right thumb and index finger is important and can add greatly to the clubface control. Broadly speaking, the tighter the two are together and the nearer the front of the club the thumb, the more likely the player is to fade or slice the ball and the less likely to hook it (hence club golfers with the right thumb down the front who immobilise the wrists and invariably slice.) The further the right thumb is opened round to the left, the more likely the player is to hook. It isn't a question of moving the whole hand over but of opening up the space between thumb and index finger. Exaggerating this is fairly unusual but often seen in those who hook the ball, particularly if they started as children. Ray Floyd stands out as the professional with a very open right-hand grip, thumb well round to the left. (Perhaps this contributed to his shot pulled left into the pond in that playoff with Nick Faldo in the Masters.) Certainly, for the player troubled with a slice or persistent fade opening up the spaces – more trigger and the right thumb further over – can often do the trick.

Ben Hogan, in his marvellous book *The Modern Fundamentals of Golf*, described the right thumb and index finger as being tightly united, with minimum gap between them. Hogan was previously troubled by a hook. Uniting the thumb and index finger acted to firm up the wrists and lessen the likelihood of a closing clubface.

For the tournament golfer wanting the odd drive with a suspicion of fade, bringing the right thumb a shade nearer the front of the club is often all that is needed. Pressing down a touch with the pad of the thumb can immobilise the wrists, holding the clubface a degree or two open through impact.

Opening the space between thumb and index finger creates *looseness*, with shots likely to be *long* and *left*. Tightening the space results in *stiffness* and shots that are *shorter* and tending to *slice*.

VARDON WAS RIGHT – BUT IS NICKLAUS WRONG?

There is little doubt that the Vardon grip is the best and most widely taught. Indeed, there are many top teachers, including me, who feel that the interlocking grip is substantially wrong. And yet, how can one say this when it is used by both Jack Nicklaus and Nancy Lopez? If the best man golfer of his generation and best woman golfer of her generation both use it, surely it has its merits?

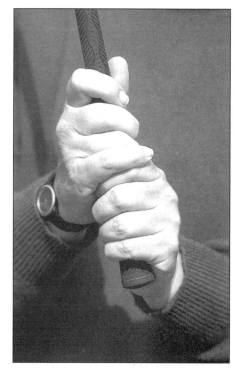

An easier version of the Vardon grip for those with small hands, little finger resting on top of the index finger

The problem with the interlocking grip is that it has only six fingers on the club. The Vardon grip has seven; the baseball eight. The baseball grip may lack bonding and be liable to change. It gives plenty of strength to those with small or weak hands, and plenty of leverage with the right for those prone to slicing. For a good player it just gives a hint of inconsistency.

The Vardon grip overcomes this. The most orthodox version is for the little finger of the right hand to fit between the index finger and second of the left. This requires a right hand with plenty of spread, right index finger triggered away from the next, little finger easily separated from the third. An easier version, but just as good, is to sit the little finger on top of the index finger. It requires less spread, easier as one gets older or for those with small hands or a short little finger. Either way, the hands are united.

The drawback of the interlocking grip is that it takes the left index finger off the club. This is the strongest finger of the left hand. For the right-handed golfer the left hand usually needs all the power it can muster. Take the left index finger off the club and perhaps 40 percent of the finger strength is lost. Any pro using the Vardon grip will use the left index finger to control many of the touch shots – the punches and pitches, the bunker shots and cut shots. With the interlocking grip the finger strength is wasted – perhaps, one might suggest, why Nicklaus always rated his bunker play the weakest part of his game.

The real merit of the interlocking grip is that it sets the beginner in a position where his hands are locked together and less likely to wander. The drawback is that he gradually shifts out of position. Instead of just interlocking the finger tips he begins to lock the fingers for their full length. The whole of the index finger becomes visible hanging out at the back. The left hands slips round to the left in a weak position and the right hand under to the right in a strong position. The player is likely either to hook or to slice, or both! The grip shows no cohesion of the left thumb sitting in the palm of the right hand.

The general theory has been that, because Jack Nicklaus uses the interlocking grip and has small hands, it is good for players with small hands. In fact it is probably more suited to a very strong man, or perhaps a left-

Jack Nicklaus – finger **tips** interlocked

Wrong. The club golfer usually interlocks too much of the fingers, allowing both hands to slide too much under the club

Olazabal with the weakest of left-hand grips. One which for many would result in the left hand failing to stand up to the right – sometimes producing a hook where the theory books say it should slice!

hander playing right-handed, who can afford to have the left index finger off the club.

In changing to the Vardon grip from the interlocking the pupil usually wants to form the right-hand grip starting with the little finger being placed in position. He is obsessed with where it fits. Correctly the other three fingers should first be placed in position, with the little finger relaxing and finding its own natural resting place.

The interlocking grip is potentially so clumsy; the Vardon grip is far more elegant. The little finger just hangs out and relaxes. Perhaps explaining why all members of very smart golf clubs drink their tea with the little finger protruding just a touch. The interlocking grip just isn't tradition!

WEAK GRIP AND STRONG GRIP – THEORY AND PRACTICE

As all good golfers know, a weak grip is one in which the Vs between the thumb and index finger of either or both hands point to the chin or left of it, encouraging a slice. A strong grip is where the Vs – one or both – point to the right shoulder or outside it, leading the player to hook. In theory this is what happens. This is how pros demonstrate the faults. That, indeed, is how most club golfers react with a poor grip.

But theory and practice are not always the same. The good golfer with a strong grip may not hook. He may push or even fade the ball. Subcon-

Bernhard Langer, with a very strong left hand, right hand orthodox

sciously he is a hooker; the odd hook haunts him for months. The ball leaves the clubface so fast and is the most destructive shot. He resists it and blocks the ball away to the right, perhaps keeping a strong left-hand grip and gradually weakening the right further over. Everything from address to the top of the backswing looks set to produce a draw or hook. The result can be a cut. An overly strong grip may not allow the player to release with the hands or rotate with the forearms for fear of closing the face. Weakening the left hand may encourage the player to have the feeling of trying to hook the ball, and enable him to square up the clubface. The answer to his fade or push may not therefore be strengthening the grip but weakening it – quite the opposite to what the theory books say.

Occasionally we see just the opposite – a player who hooks from a weak left-hand grip. Olazabal at times falls into this trap and Henry Cotton actually advocated weakening the left hand to draw or hook, and strengthening it to fade. The left hand fails to stand up to the power of the right. The right hand closes over through impact, the left providing minimum resistance. The player may have started out with a draw from a strong grip, weakens the grip because the books all tell him to do so, and keeps on weakening it. The hook perhaps goes into abeyance for a time and then re-emerges as the grip is weakened too far. By strengthening the left hand over a touch, the player may find himself able to attack the ball more aggressively and give the left more power to match the dominant right.

The essence of a good grip is that it delivers the clubface squarely to the ball, with speed and power. It is your link between the body and the clubface. Remember that its very purpose is to transmit feeling from the fingertips to the club-face and back again – with every club in the bag.

John Daly showing a real spread to his hands, right index finger well stretched for power, perhaps at the expense of control

2 PERFECT PREPARATION

The golf swing is like knocking in a nail. Rehearse the strike, think forwards as you draw back the hammer (or club) and return on the same path

For a tournament golfer the most important part of the swing, on a day-to-day basis, is the address position. On some days you step onto the practice ground and feel good immediately. On others, everything looks the same, even to the most critical and trained of eyes, but it just doesn't feel right. No golfer, however great, ever gets to the stage where the swing feels the same day after day. Don't kid yourself that you will be any different. I once asked Bernhard Langer whether he felt changes creep into his apparently methodical game. His answer was that he goes to the practice ground and sees which swing he has woken up with that morning! Even for players such as Nick Faldo, Bernhard Langer and Seve Ballesteros, the feel from day to day can be horribly different. And it all starts at address.

For the medium-handicap player we have to teach the right position. The good golfer knows in theory how to address the ball. But the ball position, distance from the ball and posture can all change minutely, but sufficiently for the swing to feel on song or not. Professional golfers, not surprisingly, achieve a far more repetitive position than most amateurs. But even so, change is inevitable. Get a good, comfortable address position on the first shot of the day and this often sets the pattern for the round.

WHY ADDRESS THE BALL?

The first question is why we address the ball at all? Why not start at the top of the backswing? To some, this is the most important part of the swing, so why not start there? Why not fix your eye on the ball and simply adopt a stationary backswing position which would now, in effect, be our new address position?

The reason is that whenever we aim at striking an object we usually start with a rehearsal of the strike.

You don't usually hit a nail with a hammer without starting with the hammer by the nail. You rehearse the feeling of and position for hitting it, draw back the hammer and give the nail a thump. The golf swing works on the same principle. Or does it?

Address should be a forward feeling rehearsal of impact, but with hips and shoulders square – not just preparation for the backswing

The address position should be a rehearsal of the impact position. We rehearse the strike, we draw back away from it and return to it. The more similar the address position and impact the better, as a rule, the swing will be. In reality, the legs and hips will be a touch more turned towards the target by impact, but essentially there is a return to the same position. The feeling at address should be of posing the impact position for a photograph – some even suggest with the hips a touch open, to produce the exact 'impact'. From here, the swing turns and returns to this position and then swings on through.

But for many, the feelings of a hammer striking a nail and the golf club about to strike a ball are worlds apart. The reason lies in the thought process. With a hammer knocking in a nail sideways, your thought is a forward one. With the golf swing, if you aren't careful, so much emphasis goes on swinging the club back that the brain works in the wrong direction.

V.J. Singh – a tall player with good posture not just for the backswing but for the finish

Wrong. The danger for the tall golfer is of squatting at address, promoting a flat feeling to the backswing but with no room for the legs to work through to a finish

The address position should always have a 'forward press'. This is a concentration of the mind and muscles towards the target. But the forward press is often better if mental rather than visible. If visible it can lead to minute changes in the grip or too much opening of the hips or shoulders. If purely mental, it is a summoning up of forward thoughts and of the delivery position to which you want to return.

The impact with the ball is the most important moment of the swing. The address is a forward-feeling rehearsal of that moment.

POSTURE AT ADDRESS

Working on the philosophy that the address position must feel good for both swinging back and swinging forwards, let's start with posture. If the address position is seen only as preparation for going backwards, the posture can easily show faults. The taller the player, the more likely the problems. A good address position should encourage the player to swing into the correct backswing. But equally, from an address position the feeling should be of being able to make a good through-swing and follow-through without a preliminary backswing. The tall golfer will often crouch at address, squatting with the knees. This promotes the feeling of a flattish, shallow backswing, which he may see as the key to good golf. It may, however, if he focuses his brain forward, show quite clearly that it is an unsuitable position from which to move forwards with ease.

There are two aims from good posture. The first is to create the correct back angle to be maintained throughout. The second is to create space for the left leg to work correctly through impact and to promote good balance.

BOTTOM UP, SCORES DOWN!

In the correct posture the bending should be from the hips and not the waist. High hips promote a flat angle to the lower back which can be maintained from start to finish. They also give space for the left leg to work through.

To create good posture, start by standing with *relaxed* legs – like standing watching a golf tournament or in the queue at the supermarket. The legs are relaxed, not bent. But nor are they rigid and locked in their sockets. From here, simply bend from the hips, keeping the lower back fairly flat. Feel the same in the legs as standing upright and they will take up their natural flex to balance the body. If you are tall playing a short iron, they will appear bent. If short and playing a driver, they will appear straight. But they are essentially relaxed. From this posture, they don't necessarily stay relaxed. Tension may be added to build resistance in the swing, but the posture itself follows these lines.

The legs from this view should appear relaxed, bottom up. For the tall player with a short iron the legs naturally bend, weight on the balls of the feet

The less good posture comes from bending in the waist instead of the hips. This produces a slouch – an overly bent lower back – and the legs tend to pop back and straighten. The swing will often give the impression of rather stiff legs. South African John Bland and American Lanny Wadkins both show this kind of posture. (One can always take comfort from the fact that, whatever the golfing fault, there is usually some great golfer who employs it!) But the correction is not one of bending the knees to overcome the stiff legs. Instead of a slouch, bending the knees turns the posture into an S-shape, standing for the 'sit and sag' it portrays! The correction is to stick the backside out and up and flatten the lower back.

With the correct posture, the lower back should feel fairly straight without being unnecessarily tense. By the end of the swing, the back angle remains virtually constant, minimising any twisting. The tall golfer will show a little more arching in the finish but still feel a constant back angle throughout.

For a small player with a driver the legs are straighter, weight more towards the heels

MAKING SPACE FOR THE LEFT LEG

Good balance is one of the most critical elements of a good technique. Without it the player has an urge, whether conscious or subconscious, to get the swing over and done with before he falls over. The better the balance, the easier the timing. As with almost all sports, those who balance well seem to have so much time, to be so unrushed.

From impact the swing must turn on through into a position which is perfectly balanced on the left leg. If the leg is bowed and bent, forcing weight onto the outside of the foot, balance is usually a struggle. This throws pressure onto the back, with a swing which doesn't always last. Correctly the left leg should be reasonably straight in the finish, with the balance on the back two-thirds of the foot. The balance is like an ordinary standing position – not the address position. Let's go back to standing watching a tournament. The legs are relaxed and you can wiggle your toes in your shoes. Pressure isn't on the toes to keep your balance. By the end of the swing, the balance should be the same. The hips should turn through to face the target, the left foot still in its address position but with the left leg fairly straight and the hips cleared. In the correct position you can wiggle the toes of the left foot. The weight shouldn't be concentrated on the ball of the left foot, possibly even curling up the toes

Seve with characteristic bowed left leg through impact. Often the result of a slightly squatting posture at address, and a movement which can put the back under great stress

with the struggle not to fall over. The balance on the left leg should be firm and comfortable. The left hip will be pushed out to the left slightly, a view from the flag seeing the hips centred over the left leg. The left leg doesn't stretch vertically; it should be straight but sinking onto the straight left leg, balanced virtually over the heel. The taller the player the harder this is to achieve.

The address position needs to promote this feeling. Squatting may make the backswing feel great but the throughswing feel awful. So from address, with the thoughts going firmly forwards, the address position should have a feel of encouraging good balance. Make an address, swing

through. Repeat it. Does the left leg seem to have space? The taller golfer with a short iron still needs the feeling of keeping the hips high and standing close enough to the ball to encourage this. If the hips drop, space for the left leg is lost and the knee buckles.

So, first find an address position which feels good in a forward-feeling direction – a mental forward press, posture encouraging a constant back angle and a hip position promoting balance and space for the left leg.

ABOVE: Good posture promotes good balance, weight on the back two-thirds of the left foot in the finish, toes working free

LEFT: Nick Faldo giving himself space for the left leg to straighten (not stiffen) through impact

Posture should always be set before gripping the club with both hands, encouraging consistent aiming and distance from the ball

POSTURE FIRST – GRIP AND DISTANCE FOLLOW

Posture problems for club golfers often arise through the player making too definite a decision on how far he is going to stand from the ball before assuming the correct posture. He is then usually too far away, holds the club out at arm's length and shoulder height and then lowers himself and the club to the ball. This wrongly leads the player to extend the arms forwards and hence to round the shoulders. As he lowers himself to the ball he usually bends from the waist, rounds the shoulders and gets the upper back into too stooped and dominant a position.

The only way of gripping the club really well while standing upright is to relax the arms down to the front and to hold the club vertically or virtually horizontally but with the arms at waist height. In this way the shoulders are relaxed down, not pulled forwards.

In approaching the ball the posture should start to take shape before the club is gripped with both hands. There should be a slight bending from the hips. The club is held in the right hand and set behind the ball, the posture is adopted and the left hand added, preferably all merging together. From here the feet can move backwards and forwards with a little flexibility until the perfect distance is found. Posture first – grip and distance follow.

ARM POSITION FOR CLEARANCE AND RELAXATION

The arms also need to be set in a position which encourages both a good backswing and throughswing. In the main it is the backswing with which we are now concerned. The arms must be set in a position from which they most easily move to the top of the backswing. The left will stay straight, though not rigid, with the right folding away smoothly. They create this relationship at address. But, ever mindful that we are rehearsing the strike, the feeling must again be like our posed impact – not contorted or overly rigid with the left, not unnecessarily dropped and tucked in with the right. But the arms must have clearance; they must be above the chest. The left must never sit too relaxed round the side of the body. It must have a clear passage to the top of the backswing. In the simplest of backswings the only feeling needed may be of the left arm drawing across and up towards the right shoulder. For the right-handed golfer, the left arm may always need encouragement to work, with just the right degree of tension.

But, again, with the through-swing in mind the left must also be in a position from where it can fold out of the way. The elbow bone should never face the target at impact. Just as the right folds in the backswing, so the left must fold away in the throughswing. The elbow begins to point to the hip. So it must at address. The left arm needs clearance with just the right degree of firmness and energy, but at address it must also show its desire to fold away. The inside of the left arm should be visible but not contorted and twisted. The left hand is brought over sufficiently in the grip by turning from the wrist, not the whole arm. Club golfers aiming at strengthening the grip often then err on the side of bringing the arm over, encouraging a blocked arm through impact.

The arm position at address, giving clearance for the arms above the chest, inside of the arms looking forward, right shoulder and arm naturally below the left

Frank Nobilo – a classic swing where address and impact match perfectly, club and hands returning through their starting points

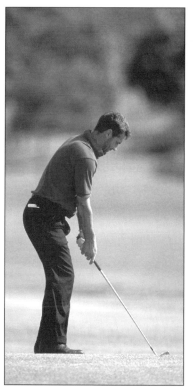

Higher handicaps then leave the clubface open; better golfers block the arm and roll the wrists for a hook. A simple check is to hold the club at address and be able to lift it by folding from the elbows. If the elbows point out, the arms can't bend.

The position of the arms should once again rehearse the feeling of impact. How high or low do the wrists sit at address? They may not necessarily come through the same place at impact, but ideally they should. If the hands start lower at address than they arrive at impact, this is a sure sign of the swing coming off plane or of some compensatory movement. The speed of the delivery may see the hands rise a touch. For this reason the correct lie of a club at address gives enough room to fit a smallish coin under the toe. By impact the sole is flush to the ground. But the change is minimal; the whole angle of the shaft should not change substantially. Watch Ian Woosnam at address and impact. The club matches precisely. Look at Paul Azinger and a substantial change takes place, with the hands coming down on a far higher path. Not wrong, just more complicated.

Again, our key is the feeling of a posed photo of impact.

SHORTENING THE RIGHT SIDE

The right hand is below the left on the club. The right shoulder must be below the left at address and impact. Here again, feelings of discomfort can arise from day to day. The feeling is simply of shortening the right side of the body from shoulder to hip and slightly lengthening the left. Novices find it unnatural. Problems can also arise for good golfers in two particular situations. The first applies to those who are tall with relatively narrow shoulders – often young boys or tall women. The shoulders may easily get too level. The second likely source of error is if the ball is played too far forwards in the stance. Suddenly the right shoulder doesn't want to sit below the left but tends to come up and forwards. A combination of build and ball position needs watching.

Once again, a rehearsal of impact is often the clue. But – and here is the rub – the easier the player finds it to achieve the correct shoulder line for the long game, the more he may find problems with pitching and the short game. For, where the golden rule with the long game is to ease the right shoulder below the left, the key for the short game is a high right shoulder from start to finish. How perverse is the game we play!

HANGING THE CLUB AT ADDRESS

For those with a quick swing, one of the problems is to ensure that the takeaway is smooth without spoiling the timing. Some players, like Jack Nicklaus, have a very slow, deliberate takeaway, gradually creating momentum through the backswing. Others, such as Tom Watson or Nick Price, have a very quick back and through action – one, two, with no gradual crescendo. It is no good trying to change a punchy player into a 'slowly back' type of player. Just as one athlete has a short, punchy run-up with his jump or throw and another a far longer build-up, so we have to keep our natural timing.

But the quick swinger can become jerky and lose his timing. One essential ingredient of the preparation is to ensure that the club is *hanging* from the arms and shoulders. The weight of the club must be supported by you and not by the ground. Sometimes players striving to relax sit the club on the ground behind the ball, give the impression of gripping it correctly but in reality don't have the weight of the club in their hands. Just as the takeaway starts, the player has to gather its weight before swinging it back. This can go hand in hand with tension and a little lift of the shoulders. It can result in too quick or steep a take-away or poor clubface control. The attempt to relax produces a sudden build up of tension. Instead the club can touch the grass with a fairway shot or hover fractionally above the ground with a tee shot for control and smoothness. Again, go back to the impact rehearsal and feel in control.

A FIRM BASE

The golf swing requires a coiling action in the backswing, like winding up a spring. To make a coil effective, one end has to be trapped and firm. In the good player's golf swing power is created by working against the resistance and tension of the legs. It all starts from the feet and knees. They, in effect, should feel firmly planted in the backswing, or, if they move, provide resistance against being pulled from their starting point.

The position of the feet needs to be repetitive. The right should be virtually straight in front. Club golfers often let the right foot wander out. It allows a turn, but a turn too loose for the aspiring champion, and if turned out more than an inch or so it immobilises the legs for the throughswing. The left foot should be turned out a touch more. It must allow the hips to turn through to the target in the throughswing without inhibiting the coil of the backswing. The feet should be wider than the knees – shoulder width for men, hip width for women. In this way the knees are knocked in a shade and always narrower than the feet. Providing this is the case there need be no feeling of pointing in the left knee on the backswing; it moves naturally. If anything the weight is slightly on the inside of the feet at address. For many players the right knee to foot will seem to be the pivot around which the whole coil takes place.

The feet should feel strong and active, balanced perhaps on the balls of the feet for the tall player and with an iron, more towards the heels for a smaller player and with a wood. They should feel as though the weight wants to move forwards on the ball of the left foot in the backswing, with the right knee – indeed both knees resisting – and then back onto the left heel in the throughswing.

DO YOUR EYES DECEIVE YOU?

What we think we do in the golf swing and what we actually do are often very different. Our eyes can play tricks on us. It starts with the club itself.

Those of us who have played for many years take it for granted that the clubface must be square. And yet, in reality, the starting point may not be a square face. Colouring the bottom grooves of irons makes them eye-catching and often assists in setting the club squarely. The problem for good golfers is often with offset clubs. The whole idea of an offset club is that it discourages the club player from slicing. It sets the hands further ahead of the clubface. But it also leads most players to set the face shut. The instinct is to line up the toe and the hosel instead of the leading edge. Suddenly the toe is turned in and the face shut. This is our first optical illusion.

The second is the positioning of the ball on the clubface. Again we take it for granted that the ball is in the middle of the clubface. But if you position the ball to look central in the face from your address position and then walk round behind it, the ball is usually nearer the heel than you imagine. For the good player this causes few problems. If we do address it towards the neck we usually make an inside attack and pull it back to the sweet spot. But the club golfer is often beset with a shank. This doesn't cause, but certainly aggravates, the problem. With some novices the ball comes so repeatedly from the neck that it simply scuttles along the ground, giving the impression that the shot is topped when it is in fact shanked. There, then, is our second illusion – more the problem of the club golfer than of the expert.

The third is in aiming. Many players simply don't see a straight line accurately from ball to target. This can run right through the whole game from driving to putting, and for the whole of a player's career.

The easiest way of aiming is to stand directly behind the ball, to choose a spot just ahead of it and in line with the hole and to aim the clubface and stance over and parallel to this. The difficulty is that in looking up, the aiming may feel wrong. The player doesn't trust it and adjusts the feet. The key to doing this correctly is to ensure that while walking round to take up the stance there is not only a clear picture of the spot but also a clear picture in the head of the target. Then, having adopted the correct address position and still thinking of the chosen spot, the picture of the target is clear and vivid. The shot can either be played without looking up again or, if another look is made, there is more likelihood of trusting the stance. The feeling is of hitting out over the spot towards the picture of the target.

Remember that you don't hit a ball to the target. You can't see the target at the moment of impact. You hit it to *the picture in your head* of the target – a very different proposition.

Far more players err on the side of aiming right than left. The first is usually an optical illusion; the second simply a reaction to slicing. The error and distortion may arise from trying to judge a straight line to the target without the eyes being directly above the ball and line. But the same error follows with putting. Here is an exercise to check your natural tendencies. Work first on the putting green and then extend the process to the long game. Line up three spots on a flat green – a ball, a marker some 18 inches ahead of it and a tee peg 6 feet away. Do this from behind the line. Now adopt your address position. The three points may no longer appear in a straight line. If the marker appears displaced to the left, your natural tendency is to aim to the right of it and to the right of the hole. The same will invariably follow with the long game. With a ball, the spot and a flag lined up from behind, the spot may seem wrong from your address position. If seemingly displaced left, your tendency is to aim right – the more common of the two.

If aiming is a problem – and it is for many – practice must always simulate what you face on the course. It is no good setting a club down and lining up along this. You can't do that on the course. Each shot must be meticulously aimed, and the feet, if necessary, then checked. Any errant shot on the course should be checked afterwards. Hold the follow-through, return the right foot to address and then lay the club down to get feedback from which to learn.

But remember that in aiming it is not just the feet that are important. The shoulders in many ways have much more bearing on the swing. If the clubface and the shoulders are square the swing has every chance of success; an error in foot position can be of little consequence. But mis-align the shoulders, particularly if the right shoulder is up and open, and the chance of success fades.

Jack Nicklaus – club hanging at address for a smooth takeaway, ball **not** opposite the left heel

BALL POSITION – REALITY AND ILLUSION

Of all the problems affecting professional golfers the ball position is one of the most difficult. For many professional tournament players, getting the ball slightly out of position is the most likely source of discomfort. Shots may be just a little lacklustre. A feeling of uncertainty begins to creep in. Is the ball an inch too far forward or an inch too far back? The error in the shots may be the same – perhaps a little drift away to the right. One of the problems is seeing your own ball

A study of address – Payne Stewart and Lee Janzen – the ball position with the drive not as far forward as is often suggested

position. Where you think you position it and where you in fact position it may be quite different. The best way of checking is to lay down a club with the head around the left foot or to ask for a second opinion.

A frequently suggested theory is that all shots should be played from just inside the left heel, whether with driver or wedge, the stance simply narrowing with the right foot through the set of clubs. Most instructional books from the 1960s to the 1980s make this suggestion. And yet, in practice, this ball position does not suit everyone. If the ball is played this far forward it requires, for most, a great deal of leg action to make a good contact with the ball. There is a tendency for the left leg to bow out and for the hips to tip and tilt through impact. If the ball is played well forwards the line of the shoulders can begin to open, and the swing starts aiming left through impact. But even for players who do work to this theory – Jack Nicklaus for example – the ball isn't going to be played from this position from a tight or downhill lie. The golden rule is to position the ball where it encourages the desired contact, combined with good direction to the attack. As a general rule, more problems are likely to be encountered by playing the ball too far forwards than playing it too far back. If the ball is marginally too far back it at least encourages an inside attack and ball-divot strike with an iron.

For most golfers the natural bottom of the swing does not fall opposite the left instep or heel; it falls a couple of inches further back. By struggling to collect the ball from too far forwards there tends to be excessive movement, either with the legs driving forward or the shoulders coming over.

Many tournament golfers say they position the ball opposite the left heel, but they don't. They think they do. It is an illusion. The aspiring tournament player copies this, producing sloppy leg action or finding his contact and penetration with shots less than perfect.

A more logical approach is to position the ball 2 to 3 inches inside the left heel. At this point most golfers make a better contact and also more easily attack it from the inside. It does, of course, depend on the width of the stance. Perhaps the main change David Leadbetter made with Nick Faldo's swing was to pull the ball further back. This allowed Nick to firm up the left leg through impact and to produce a more solid strike. It also made possible a shallower turn of the shoulders, encouraging a flatter plane to the backswing. It is also worth noting how many tournament pros play a driver or 3-wood more centrally in the stance than they and most golfers imagine.

For the medium- and higher-handicap player, playing the ball too far forward in the stance before the technique allows restricts a good shoulder turn. Visually it becomes very difficult to turn the shoulders and still see the ball comfortably; the swing starts becoming an up-and-down action. It is crucial for the higher-handicap player to learn his golf with the ball not far ahead of centre. This encourages a turn, not a lift. Only when he can achieve an inside attack should he edge the ball forwards towards the left heel.

Again, the eyes can deceive. We don't always see our own ball position. We don't always know where it should be.

DISTANCE FROM THE BALL – USE A YARDSTICK

The question almost every beginner asks is how far he should stand from the ball. It is impossible to give a clear-cut answer. It varies, of course, with height, posture, the lie and through the set of clubs. The beginner continually has doubts about the position. The best advice is just to position the hands somewhere under the chin, but with the arms hanging clear of the chest. We give comfort by saying that it will soon become natural.

In reality, of course, it never does become natural! Most good golfers have problems at one time or another with finding the right distance from the ball. Like the ball position it is a very sensitive thing, varying a little from day to day and often causing the feelings of comfort or discomfort which may determine the ease or difficulty of each round.

For top-class players the golf swing tends to go in a cycle. We reach a crescendo where everything feels brilliant, and we try to stay with that feeling and at that level for as long as possible. The feeling then starts to deteriorate and drop backwards. Eventually we reach rock bottom, make some minor adjustment, and lift ourselves back towards normality. For some, the feelings of being at one's best and being at rock bottom may be tantalisingly close! The difference between Tom Watson at his very best and Tom

Watson at rock bottom is almost imperceptible, while the difference for some players may be alarmingly noticeable. It is essential for the player to know what takes him out of the feeling of supremacy and starts allowing the swing to deteriorate. It is then a question of picking things up as quickly as possible and not allowing things to decline too far. With most top-class golfers it is a question of finding just the right feeling at address. A player perhaps performs to his best and then creeps just that little bit too far away from the ball or allows the ball to get too far forward in the stance. It is all too easy to back further away from the ball with a subconscious feeling of over-confidence. The direction of the swing then begins to deteriorate. It may be just fractional but enough to distinguish best from less than best.

So how do we find a position that can be reproduced? The problem is that we stand on a variable surface and have so many clubs to deal with. If you stand below the ball you have to stand further from it; if you stand above it you have to stand closer. There are elements of variation which we cannot control. We cannot mark our position like the run-up of a long-jumper or the bowler in cricket. We have to rely on eye and judgement.

Out on the course we have two things to rely on. The first is how we feel – that elusive feeling which can change marginally from day to day. The other is the look of things. How do our hands and feet look in relation to each other as we look down on them? Both can be used to give us a clue to the right position. Ideally, of course, we would always stand to the ball and feel perfect. But that simply doesn't happen. So how about the view of it? Supposing we set up with a driver, feeling comfortable. We look down and see the view of our feet, our hands, the end of the grip and so on? What sort of triangle does it form? Do we see a straight line between left toes, end of the grip, right toes and so on? Is our weight distribution spot-on to give that position? (This can be a clue, not so much for the top-class golfer but for the low- and medium-handicap golfer whose ball position and distance from the ball may vary by several inches.) Are the hands comfortably under the chin or do they get thrown further forward?

In practice we must have some standard to go back to. I am a great believer in any aspiring golfer going out on the practice range with a metre ruler and actually measuring the precise ball position with the driver and a 5-iron when things feel good. Do take measurements: the distance between my big toes is – so many inches; the distance between that line and the ball is – so many inches, etc. Make a note of the distances and use them as a reference. Don't think this is too precise. Many golfers spend thousands of pounds on golf equipment and lessons, pace off distances and so on and then are afraid of being seen working to such technical margins on the practice ground. We still have to reproduce this feeling on the course, but at least we have something to go back to. We can focus on how it felt when things were going well and reproduce that precise position.

As an alternative take a large sheet of newspaper, stand on it and mark off your ball position and foot position for a driver and a 5-iron. Keep it as a reference: 'Playing brilliantly, 5 September 1994!'

To sum up, distance from the ball is crucial, variable and often rather illusory. The key throughout is to remember that address is a rehearsal of impact, like knocking a nail in a wall. Think forwards. Turn and return.

GROOVING THE BACKSWING

THE WHOLE SWING

Peter Baker showing the simplest of swings. Rehearse the feeling of impact at address, turn away from it with a lift of the arms, return through impact on the same path and move into a perfectly controlled and balanced finish. What could be simpler than that?

Before embarking on the quest for knowledge about the swing, it is important to see it as a whole. What are we trying to achieve? Good teaching should see the entire golf swing, never losing sight of its true aims, before breaking it down into pieces. The aim of the swing is to hit the ball as reliably as possible from A to B. It must stand up to tiredness, pressure, moods, bad weather – and preferably last a lifetime.

Golf is a stationary ball game. Racquet players usually suggest that a moving ball game is far easier. A stationary ball poses problems. The essence of the golfing novice's problems is that he is faced with a ball which is too small and a clubhead which is too small. The ball sits on the ground and the ground gets in the way! Contact is far harder than in most other games. Perhaps the only sport more difficult for the beginner is cricket, in that the worse you are the fewer hits you get, with little chance of improvement. At least the worse you are with golf, the more goes you get!

But that aside, the stationary ball does cause problems. It just sits there, giving too much time for thought. Many golfers would play better if the ball popped up, sat still for 5 seconds and had to be struck within that time.

Movements would have to be spontaneous, with less time for over-thinking.

High-speed photos tend, to some, to be a menace. They can lead golfers to see too many 'positions' in the swing. They are analysed and copied too thoroughly, very often destroying the body's natural coordination and rhythm.

Another danger is of teaching professionals trying to focus on ever more detailed parts of the swing. The student can be tempted to put his faith in the professional who sees the most intricacies and complexities. The more he is baffled by technicalities, the more he believes in the professional's knowledge of the swing. In reality the aim must be to make the swing as *simple* as possible. Playing the wretched game is hard enough! A good golf swing must always be seen as a whole – a backswing and throughswing blending together as one or two movements. The art of improving technique is to focus on large or small parts of that whole, pinpointing them and perfecting them, and then replacing them in the swing. Each needs to be moulded on the practice ground and then repeated until it becomes second nature.

As far as possible the swing should be a forward-feeling process, with the mind focused firmly on propelling the ball to the target. The whole essence of a good golf swing is to deliver the clubface squarely to the ball, at speed, with the depth, direction and angle of attack you desire. In its simplest terms, it becomes 'turn, turn, whack it and balance'! And that is what we are after – removing all the fiddly bits and developing the simplest swing possible.

Remember that analysing movement and learning movement are not the same. Simple, everyday movements would become impossible with too much thought. Pick up a teaspoon, take some sugar from a bowl and stir it into your coffee. Simple. Start to analyse every movement of every part of the body and it achieves nothing. Parts that worked naturally to balance and coordinate the movements of others are soon lost. One reason for this is that here we aren't looking for precision, speed or elegance. But there is another. With the teaspoon, we focus on it – the spoon. We move it, but it in a way controls us. We want the spoon to perform a certain function; it leads our body to work in a certain way.

In golf, the danger is of losing all sight of moving the club and the clubface. Body awareness tends to come from over-thinking. We lose the natural feel of the tool in our hands. And yet in reality it is the club and clubface which is the crucial factor. Feel it, move it and let the body move in response. Gifted, world-class golfers and most youngsters do this automatically. The danger is of those not quite so naturally gifted destroying all the natural *feel* in an effort to analyse.

Whatever your thoughts on the swing, clubface feel and the desire to move the ball from A to B must never be lost. Here then, are some concepts for the whole swing, giving a framework into which all other golfing knowledge can be slotted.

SIMPLICITY AND THE PLANE

The swing, in its simplest terms, is a turn of the body with a swishing up and down of the arms. We start at address, which is a rehearsal of impact. We move away from this by turning the back to the target and lifting the arms. From there we return to impact (having already rehearsed it at address) and then move onto a balanced follow-through, body facing the target, club over the left shoulder. Ideally most of the feeling for the delivery is created at address. Any thoughts for the backswing are enhanced in the takeaway. Preferably, by the time the club has moved back 18 inches, the rest of the backswing free-wheels itself to our desired 'position' and the brain is firmly in the forward mode for the attack.

Olazabal and the perfect plane. The angle of the clubshaft at address shows the plane of the swing. The left arm moves into this angle at the top of the backswing, the club returns through its initial angle through impact and then moves smoothly into the same angle in the finish

To see the swing in its simplest terms needs an understanding of the plane of swing. Let the club lead the way. In the most basic of methods the plane of the swing follows the club shaft at address. By the top of the backswing the left arm follows much the same angle. The club returns through its starting point at impact and then moves into a follow-through with the club shaft on the same plane. Obviously there is a degree of lift in both back-swing and follow-through, but this, basically, is what we see and like to see in the easiest of golf swings. The same follows through the set of clubs. The short irons sit with an upright lie; the swing should follow this pattern and plane. The driver sits with a flatter lie; again, the swing should follow it. Whether standing on a flat lie or above or below the ball, the golden rule is the same. In this way, the club does the minimum of twists and turns en route.

The two halves of the swing match. The planes of backswing and throughswing follow each other. It is no good putting Bernhard Langer's backswing with Greg Norman's follow-through. The two don't go together. The club would be off plane. If the plane of follow-through doesn't match that of the backswing there is some complexity along the line. The good golfer's swing shows the same pattern in the finish as at address. Working at the plane of follow-through will often sort out clubface errors through impact. Don't simply see the follow-through as the result of a good swing and shot. Aiming at a good follow-through helps promote a good delivery. Working at a repetitive follow-through, even after the ball has gone, helps the next shot and the next, and so on.

Remember that there are two ways of becoming a better golfer. The simple one is to learn to do your best swing more often, preferably every time. Make your best swing 95 per cent of the time instead of 65 per cent and you will undoubtedly improve. The more difficult, and sometimes unnecessary, route is to change your best swing. Concentrate on producing a steady, perfectly balanced and totally repeatable follow-through and this is often the key to improved performance, simply by increasing the player's number of perfect swings.

So, although like most books this starts with the backswing and works onward to the follow-through, don't underestimate the importance of the finish. See the swing as having two perfectly stationary positions – the address position and the finish. Work at those two stationary positions, perfect them and see repetition as your main aim for scoring consistency.

SIMPLICITY – LEFT ARM TO RIGHT SHOULDER

There are many concepts for encouraging a good backswing. Some people do it naturally, while to others the backswing is a constant source of problems. Remember, however, that the backswing is simply preparation for the throughswing. Tennis players are far less concerned about how they swing the racquet back than through; they see the game as a forward movement. In golf, on the other hand, many players become so bogged down with their backswing that they never learn to move through correctly.

Not every player gets in the same position. Not every player *wants* to get in the same position. There are many different types of golf swing. The thought process for Jack Nicklaus is totally different from that of Lee Trevino or Bernhard Langer. It is a question of determining your own swing type and the thoughts that mean something to your particular game.

The simplest way of tackling the backswing is to stand in a good address position, knees slightly flexed and a little knocked in towards each other, and to focus very much on the left shoulder and left arm. The simplest feeling of all for a perfect backswing is to think of swinging the left arm back and across the chest with a suspicion of lift. The feeling is one of anchoring your feet and knees and simply moving the whole unit of left arm and left shoulder towards and slightly above the right shoulder. The left shoulder does not in fact move above the right but often needs to *feel* a suspicion of lift. From a good grip the wrists will usually hinge correctly, and this in itself gives the simplest look to the backswing and is undoubtedly the easiest feeling to achieve.

To be able to produce this, the player must be able to work the left arm fairly tightly towards the right shoulder. To check this, simply hold your left arm out in front of you at shoulder height, palm of the hand downwards. Put the fingers of the right hand behind your left elbow and draw the arm gently across your chest towards your right shoulder. Ideally for the simplest of golf swings, there should be enough flexibility for the left arm to touch the right shoulder. In the swing, of course, it won't. It is a question of suppleness, I suspect, in the back of the left shoulder and not having too ample a chest to get in the way.

If this movement feels comfortable, it can be translated very simply into the golf swing. Take up your address position, without a club, and hang the left arm down in front of you, palm facing diagonally downwards towards the right foot. Simply swing the left arm up towards the right shoulder, making sure that if anything it moves above the shoulder and never below. This, for many professionals, is all the backswing feels to be. You focus on the left arm, *feel* as though you keep the legs and knees still and simply swing the club up and across with the left arm and left shoulder. Providing the arm works fairly tightly across towards the shoulder there probably need be no particular emphasis on turning.

Woosnam, Singh and Watson. In the simplest of backswings the knees are knocked in a touch at address, the left arm and shoulder turn with a suspicion of lift, coiling everything against the resistance of the legs. The posture and hip angle stay constant (and would remain so through to impact). The wrists work naturally

With your club in your left hand, feel exactly the same movement. Simply swing the club up and across, steadying the club on the left thumb. Now add the right hand and repeat precisely the same exercise, once again almost trying to immobilise the legs and simply focusing on the left side. The knees will move. The hips will move. But they don't feel as if they're moving.

Remember that turning with the right side and turning with the left side are not the same. At address the shoulders should adopt an easy, natural position, neither rounded forward nor arched back. By the time we get to the top of the backswing the left side closes round against the right with the shoulders in a rounded position. As we will see later, one of the keys to starting the downswing is to open the left side away from the right. In the backswing it is a feeling of moving the left side round against the right side, left arm working across and towards the right. If by contrast you think of turning away with the right shoulder, it tends to open the shoulders, right elbow flying and chest expanding.

The easiest way of *feeling* the backswing is simply to concentrate on the left arm. For many players this simple concept will produce a perfect swing. For others it is insufficient; but this is what we are working towards. We want to get rid of all the fiddly bits until eventually the backswing simply feels like one uncomplicated movement. You set up to the ball, you turn or turn and lift with the left arm, and the rest of the body moves in sympathy with it.

FOLD THE BODY TO CREATE POWER

My concept of a coiled backswing for the good golfer is of the body folding like a piece of card. It has two distinct halves – above the hips and below the hips. It bends at that point. The top half is then divided in two. Having bent from the hips at address it is as though the top half of the body works against the resistance of the legs and lower half. The feeling is of the feet, knees and hips staying still (they don't, but they feel as though they do). The top half turns against them. But it is the left side of the body that folds to the right. The right side moves very little; the left side turns onto it. The left shoulder is rounded inwards towards the right. It is never the right side opening away. The left knee is pulled in towards the right, never rolling on the inside of the left feet but being pulled round against its own resistance. At the top of the backswing it feels as though the top half turns against the hips. You imagine the knees and hips have stayed still. You look down and are surprised to see their movement.

Having folded the left side of the body towards the right, the feeling in the downswing is then of the left side opening away again – left arm, left shoulder, left knee, leg and hip. It is almost as though the pelvis itself has folded, with the left side feeling to unwind away again. In this way resistance is developed in the backswing. The power of the downswing is a pulling away from this resistance.

TURN AND SQUEEZE THE HIP ANGLE – AVOID THE SWAY

Wrong. The player who sways or tilts straightens the angle in the hips, rather than keeping a bottom out position

In the correct backswing the hip angle remains constant, bottom out – turn and squeeze – head and top half naturally moving behind the ball

A common incorrect backswing position is for the hips to be too active. The hips may slide out to the right instead of turning directly away from the player. In women golfers especially, but indeed also in some men, the position can be very noticeable. The head stays still, the hips shift out to the side and the player is invariably told that he or she has a sway. When told he sways, the player usually imagines he produces a swing like Curtis Strange, who moves his head several inches from side to side. But in fact such a player doesn't sway from his top half or his head but with his hips. The more he is told that he sways, the more emphasis he puts on keeping the head still and the problem is thereby aggravated.

For a good backswing, the hip angle must stay constant. The fault here is that the hip angle changes.

At address we bend from the hips. That hip bend and overall posture should stay constant in the backswing and back again into impact. Again, rehearse impact. Turn and return with the simplest of movements. The player who sways or lifts or tilts will invariably straighten the hip angle, losing the hip bend in the backswing. Bend over with the same hip angle you would adopt at address, without a club in your hand. Simply turn your top half, feeling the hip angle retained. Let the head move slightly behind the ball as the top half turns away. Feel that the angle in the right hip is maintained. I call the exercise 'turn and squeeze'. To feel the movement, set up in an address position without a club, and put your right hand in the angle at the top of your right leg. Now turn as though making a backswing and keep squeezing that angle. The feeling, slightly exaggerated, is that of holding a tennis ball or golf ball in that angle, depending on your anatomy either with or without a hand steadying, and turning to simulate the top of the backswing, trying to keep that angle there. Automatically the top half of the body moves behind the ball. The weight transfers quite naturally onto the right side. With the feeling of turn and squeeze the hips no longer pop out to the side but will naturally turn very slightly and directly behind the player.

Another way of feeling this, again without a club, is to adopt an address position and then bend forward to touch your toes. Turn your entire body to the right. Your head simply turns and moves to the right. Now stand slightly more upright and again simply allow the top half of the body to turn. Come back to address and stand still more upright. Repeat the same exercise. That, now, is the feeling of the golf swing. The top half bends over, the angle in the hips is maintained and the top half turns. It allows the top half of the body to move naturally behind the ball. In a tall player this may be quite evident. Nick Faldo doesn't keep his head as still as Ian Woosnam. Nick obviously bends over more; in turning while retaining the hip bend, his head naturally moves behind the ball. Very, very occasionally we see a player with a slight reverse pivot. In other words, the player keeps his head perfectly still, seems to do all the right movements and perhaps almost shifts the hips back again to the left. But it is unusual, and causes few problems for the good player.

As a general rule, the top half must be allowed to move behind the ball. If told that you sway, ask whether you are swaying with your hips or with your head. The answer is nearly always hip sway. Think of this as an incorrect straightening up of the body as the backswing takes place. A negative thought such as 'don't sway' or 'don't tilt' is meaningless. Replace it with a positive thought of turning and squeezing, keeping a constant posture.

Why does it happen? Usually from over-emphasis on the head staying too still in the backswing, and perhaps playing the ball too far towards the left foot as a novice. The player then finds it difficult to turn the top half away from the ball while still comfortably seeing it.

Turn and squeeze and maintain the hip angle back to the top of the backswing and down again into impact.

TIGHT TURN OR LOOSE TURN

Ideally in the backswing the upper body should turn to form a coiled spring, left arm in a controlling position and preferably with the club shaft pointing parallel to our ball-target line. Some players, both club golfers and occasionally a top class player, will tend to turn insufficiently, picking up the club rather than moving it round behind them. For the higher handicap golfer it is often necessary to encourage a turn. The player feels wary of turning his back to the target through a feeling of insecurity. He feels more comfortable simply picking up the club with the arms and with a minimum of turn.

Club golfers and older golfers sometimes find the turn difficult. If the legs feel as though they are staying still the shoulders don't turn sufficiently.

They may not have the freedom to draw the left arm across the chest in the backswing. In this case, emphasis has to be put on turning, often allowing the left heel to be pulled from the ground and giving the hips and legs more freedom. There has to be a more definite turn of the shoulders to bring the club round on line. The player cannot get it there unless the right side of the body also moves out of the way. It may indeed require a degree of emphasis on hip turn, even if this turn is a fairly loose one.

Greg Norman showing a tightly wound backswing, bottom out, top half naturally moving behind the ball, with a downward, diagonal push through to the left knee and foot

ABOVE RIGHT: Payne Stewart with a far looser turn, freer and with less feeling or impression of coiling tension

But with the top-class player the turn must be a tightly wound position where there is resistance in the body right the way from the left foot upwards. It is as though there is a diagonal push down and out in the left foot and a winding up through the whole body. The right leg doesn't turn away in a sloppy position. The knees stay knocked in. And if the left heel is forced up, the whole of the ball of the foot stays in contact with the ground. The heel is literally forced up rather than flapping up and down lifelessly. In this way the body is coiled into action, creating potential energy for generating power in the downswing and throughswing.

Even for the top-class player this feeling of a coiling action may sometimes create an underturn. At this point the player probably has to loosen up, play a few shots, a few holes or perhaps a few rounds with a feeling of a slightly looser turn, to make sure that the turn is taking place. Then, when the swing is reasonably on song, he can go back to a feeling of tension and a coiling movement.

Unquestionably, however, there are top-class players who don't have that feeling. There are some who certainly seem to have a much looser form of turn. Payne Stewart, for example, gives less impression of a resisted, coiling action than of a more fluid, perhaps freer swing. So, indeed, did Bobby Jones. But to most top-class players the feeling is certainly one of creating just the right tension before exploding everything back through impact. Freedom and looseness need to be harnessed.

HANDS AND ARMS

Our next search is for the perfect hand, arm and wrist position at the top of the backswing. Professionals fail to agree on how and when the wrists work. The reason for this disagreement is that for some the movement is natural, for others unnatural. In many ways, the less you have to think of the backswing and the way the wrists work the better. Many a good golf swing has been ruined by thoughts of how the wrists break.

For those with the simplest of swings, the answer is that no independent wrist action is felt. The left arm simply moves to the top of the backswing and the hands work without thinking. As with many facets of the swing, shorter players often find the movement more natural than taller ones.

The easiest of feelings is a one-piece movement where the left wrist works naturally. If it happens, don't analyse it. An exercise to feel this is simply to hold your left arm out simulating address, without a club. Form a fist with the left hand, thumb to the front. Now swing the arm up to roughly backswing position. The wrist almost certainly adopts the correct position, neither arched nor cupped. In the easiest of golfing methods this is all that is felt. For some, however, achieving this position is far from straightforward and the backswing is a constant battle.

In some cases the correct wrist position requires a strengthening of the left arm and wrist. Weakness in the left arm often allows the left wrist to collapse into a cupped position. Holding a club in the left hand and swinging to the top of the backswing time and again allows a straighter, firmer back to the left hand.

LATE HIT AND EARLY HIT

At the top of a perfect backswing, we ideally see the back of the left wrist flat or almost flat, with the right wrist cocked back on itself. But why? The answer is in the delivery to the ball. We want to attack the ball from a 'late hit position' rather than an early hit position.

The term 'late hit' has nothing to do with time. We see pictures of golfers taken from the front showing a very marked cocking of the wrists approaching impact, with the club delayed and cocked upwards. It gives

the impression that a late hit is all about holding the wrists back and delaying the hands. Correctly the late hit and early hit positions are seen from behind the line of the shot. The late hit position is where the club-head is very much behind the hands seen from this view. The left wrist is arched, with the clubhead well behind it. From here, the arms can swing out to attack the ball on a shallow path. For the player who wants to use the hands, this position allows them to work with a forward delivery of power. All the strength is going in the right direction – forwards and not downwards – and the right hand can deliver all the power it likes, without a fear of the right side of the body taking over.

In the less good 'early hit' position the club attacks the ball from above and down the line of the shot. The right wrist generally shows far more cupping. The clubhead is almost directly above the player's hands as they approach hip-height in the downswing. From here the player is unable to release any power with the hands. The power is now aimed downwards rather than out and forwards. In this position the player may have the sensation of having to ease up on the ball for fear of the right hand and clubhead taking over.

An 'early attack' with the club approaching the ball from down the line' often the problem of the tall golfer and the likely result of cupped wrists at the top of the backswing

Lee Trevino with an inside attack, meeting the ball from well behind himself in a classic 'late hit' position

The problem for the tall player is to get the club sufficiently behind him to produce a late hit position. The tall golfer will usually hold his hands low at address, in other words forming more angle between the arms and club shaft. This wrist position tends to produce a cupping of the left wrist at the top of the backswing. When brought into reverse, this brings the club down to this early hit position. The player will often struggle from here to find an inside attack, tilting the hips, dropping the right shoulder and trying to force the club underneath.

The ideal late hit position tends to go hand in hand with the correct wrist angle at the top of the backswing, where the left wrist is relatively flat. Our next quest is to achieve this backswing position.

THE TRAY-CARRYING POSITION

Producing a fairly flat left wrist at the top of the backswing goes hand in hand with setting the right wrist back on itself. This encourages the late hit, a shallow attack, round and out towards the ball for maximum distance.

A good, old-fashioned exercise is to feel that the right hand gets into a tray-carrying position at the top of the backswing, in other words with the palm of the hand facing virtually upwards rather than forwards. In this position the right elbow will form a natural right angle, pointing more or less downwards, with the back of the hand cocked back. In looking for the ideal build for a top-class golfer we should see this freedom of the right wrist to bend back fully. Aspiring top-class players lacking this freedom can sometimes find difficulty in generating the power they would like.

This tray-carrying idea possibly sees the left wrist in an overly flat position with too much arching, but as a general concept it is a good one. The right elbow is down, the palm of the hand is up and as the right elbow drops back in against the side the right wrist retains its hinge.

The drawback of the exercise is that the backswing should be dominated by thoughts of the left side rather than thoughts of the right side. The left shoulder rounds in towards the right one rather than the right one opening up and away. But as a concept, blended in with thoughts of the left hand, it can certainly bear dividends for those striving for a perfect wrist position in the backswing. The danger, however, is of allowing the brain to work backwards away from the target instead of focusing forwards towards it.

Ernie Els, Nick Faldo and Tom Watson in classic flat-wristed positions at the top of the backswing, encouraging a late hit to the attack

LET THE DELIVERY DETERMINE THE BACKSWING

Finding the perfect backswing is often best achieved by rehearsing the attack position, left wrist feeling to be arched back behind the player, right hand and arm feeling able to generate power round and out towards the ball. Bouncing up from here gives the perfect backswing with the brain still thinking forwards

Players often spend too much time thinking of their backswing and insufficient time in thinking of the throughswing. Indeed, some teachers suggest that if you get to the top of the backswing correctly nothing can go wrong. I disagree with this. Perhaps it is true for the world-class champion for whom the delivery may be entirely instinctive and for whom the follow-through is completely repetitive. For the likes of Tom Watson it *could* be true, though I doubt it. But for 999 golfers out of 1000 everything can still go badly wrong even with the most perfect of backswings.

Players working at their backswing will often ask their professional, 'Now should I do this, or should I do this?', while making two backswings which they believe to be entirely different. In fact you can probably see no difference at all, and yet the feelings may be worlds apart. The danger, too, is that the player's brain is working in reverse. He is trying to hit the ball forwards towards a target and yet his brain is going in the opposite direction.

For many golfers the way of developing a good backswing, particularly in relation to the arms and hands, is to focus on the delivery into the ball. Let's draw a simple analogy. I screw up a ball of paper and throw it towards a waste paper basket a few feet away. I don't think how I swing my arm back; I simply propel the object in the direction I want. If I wanted to throw it further to the right I would aim my throw accordingly. I wouldn't think of swinging my arm back differently, but inevitably it would happen. We adjust our backswing by thinking of the delivery we want to make. The same thing happens in racquet sports.

With a player who has a steep, slightly out-to-in attack, it is all too easy to pick holes in the backswing and to focus attention on that. But if we change the delivery into the ball, forcing the player to attack it on a much shallower, inside path, he will start to take the club back differently. He doesn't have to think about it and, indeed, should still keep his thoughts going forwards.

In order to develop a perfect backswing, rehearse your attack into the ball, with the hands at hip or waist height. The left wrist should be arched a touch, the right wrist set naturally back on itself, and the clubhead well behind the hands in the late hit position. The feet should be firmly planted on the ground with the knees bent. To feel the position, have a colleague hold the clubhead away behind you and feel a steady pull against his resistance. The feeling should be of a potentially shallow attack on the ball, from where the club can swing round and out at the ball. All the power should feel concentrated on moving forwards.

Keep rehearsing this position, with a ball in front of you but at first simply feeling the potential power and direction of the attack. Hit shots from this as a stationary position. Then develop it further by hitting shots with a feeling of a restricted swing, clubhead attacking from behind you. From here, adopt the delivery position and then bounce it up to the top of the backswing and down again, feeling the flat back to the left hand and the right wrist back on itself. In this way the perfect backswing is found, not by focusing on how the club goes back but on how it will move on through. The working of the wrists should become natural, other than perhaps some thoughts on the potential power of the left hand and direction of the strike.

THE TWO-DIMENSIONAL WRIST-COCK

For those to whom the backswing and the wrist break continue to be a mystery, let's delve further. There are two ways in which our wrists can and indeed should hinge in the golf swing. Hold the club out in front of you at waist height. Hinge the wrists up and down. This is the first form of hinge-ing. Now take the club in the same position and hinge the club back against the right wrist. This is the second type of wrist break. The club golfer often uses only the first of these; the advanced golfer must use both.

To explain what happens, let's look at the swing from two angles. When we look at the swing from the front we see the club being taken back to, let's say, hip-height, preferably with the toe of the club now virtually uppermost. From there the wrists hinge on upwards, with the club supported by the left thumb. This is how we teach a beginner. The wrists simply work in an up-and-down direction. If you swing the club back to hip-height and cock the wrists upwards, the left wrist cups. The hands are now in a position from where they release and uncock downwards into impact. In reality this is insufficient for generating maximum power into the ball.

Ideally for the top-class player we want to see the other sort of wrist-cock come into action. There should be a natural and gradual blending of the right wrist hingeing back on itself while the wrists also hinge upwards on the thumbs. This has the effect of producing a far flatter back to the left wrist at the top of the backswing, with the right hand in a position more

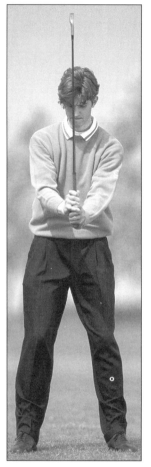

beneath the club. If from here the arms are lowered as though about to attack the ball, the right wrist is naturally set back on itself and the club shaft is behind the player's hands – our late hit position. From here there is much more ability for the right hand or right side to generate power quite naturally into the ball, for the clubhead speed to be greater and for the attack to be a shallower one.

In the simplest form of backswing, moving the left arm across and up to the right shoulder, the back of the left wrist adopts this fairly flat position. In doing this the wrists have naturally moved in two dimensions and nothing more needs to be felt. But many players find difficulty in

The golfing wrist angles – the upward hinge of the club golfer and the backward hinge of the advanced player

adding the backward hingeing. This is often the case with tall golfers who hang their arms and hands low at address, which naturally incorporates a degree of upward wrist bend from the word 'go'. As the player moves to the top of the backswing, it is this action which is likely to be the more dominant. By contrast, a player like Lee Trevino who holds his hands very high at address is more likely to hinge the wrists backwards, the left wrist being flatter at the top of the backswing. Somewhere in between the two is the optimum position from which the wrists most easily work correctly.

Particularly for the tall golfer, there often needs to be a very definite feeling of hingeing the wrists backwards in the takeaway to encourage a flatter wrist position. Nick Faldo, because of his height and hence the lower wrist position at address, builds a rehearsal of this into his set-up routine. Someone of Bernhard Langer's build usually finds it relatively simple.

The feeling of working at the delivery position sees a combination of these two wrist breaks. It begins to flatten the back of the left hand and set the right wrist back on itself for greater power.

There is great merit in strengthening the left hand, wrist and arm. As an exercise hold the club in the left hand, possibly with the thumb a touch nearer the front than normal. Swing to the top of the backswing. If the hand is weak the odds are it will collapse into a cupped position. Strengthen the position by flattening it. Work the wrist over and back, arching it and flattening it repeatedly until the muscle strength is improved. With the left more in control, the two-dimensional wrist break can start to take shape. The feeling is of hingeing the wrists backwards and cocking them upwards, blending the two together quite smoothly and naturally.

Nick Faldo practising the wrist hinge to set the club behind himself for a flat left wrist at the top of the backswing

THE OLD-FASHIONED WAGGLE

To develop the correct wrist action and late hit position, the old-fashioned waggle has its merits. For those of us learning to play golf in the 1950s or 1960s (and even earlier, of course), the good old-fashioned waggle was part of the preparation for the swing. The waggle was not just a loosening-up action; it encouraged the wrists to work in the correct way. I suppose as children we weren't taught how to waggle but I presume adults were.

The essence of a waggle was (and for its advocates it still is) to hinge the wrists backwards and forwards so that the club travelled back slightly past the right knee and returned neatly towards the ball. It was in effect training the right wrist to hinge backwards rather than to cock upwards. This preparation was all very much part of the swing. As the right wrist hinged back in making a waggle, it also meant that the right hand was being trained to get into this sort of position during the backswing and the attack. As it did so, the left wrist was naturally going to push forward and then work over into a fairly flat position at the top of the backswing with the right hand beneath.

My suspicion is that Jack Nicklaus killed the waggle. Unlike most pros in the 1960s he simply set the club motionless behind the ball, moving into the slowest of takeaways, building up a crescendo of speed. But, as the best in the world, his technique was copied. Just as the interlocking grip was born or at least popularised, the waggle became a thing of the past – certainly from a teaching point of view.

But the waggle has its merits. It gives a couple of neat little rehearsals for setting the right wrist back in the delivery position. Tom Watson is the best, with a waggle that happens precisely the same way each time. But it needs to be understood. For the player trying to get the right wrist back on itself and a flatter left wrist at the top of the backswing, the movement can be tremendously beneficial. The initial worry is that the clubhead will inadvertently touch the ball. Not so when done correctly. Correctly the clubhead moves away and round as the wrists cock backwards. Then, as the club is returned towards the ball, it is simply swept on up above it, with no danger of wobbling the ball. The movement soon becomes a totally natural one.

Look closely at many of the world's top golfers and the waggle is there. It is all about preparing for the delivery and getting the hands in the right position. It doesn't allow the player to hinge the wrists upwards into a weak position, but encourages a strong attack position early in the backswing. The feeling is of *forward* preparation – a ready position for a good delivery.

Tom Watson and a good old-fashioned waggle, training the left wrist to move back on itself in the backswing

Nick Faldo produces the same kind of movement but with a rather more methodical and perhaps contrived style. Nick's way of doing this is to make a definite forward thrusting of the back of the left wrist while hingeing the right wrist back on itself as a rehearsal to the swing. Again it is aimed at eradicating a cupped left wrist at the top of the backswing and at producing an attack from behind himself. In reality it is an overly precise version of the waggle but far more static than free. I think this approach is too contrived for most, but perhaps it will at least see the revival and understanding of the merits of a good old-fashioned waggle.

THE FALLACY OF POINTING THE CLUB 'ON LINE'

In looking at a backswing we ideally see the player in a position where the club shaft is horizontal or virtually horizontal and pointing parallel to the line of the shot. If the club shaft points away to the right of the target it may be a question of overturning in the backswing, perhaps taking the club away too much on the inside or possibly cocking the wrists loosely. If on the other hand the club points away to the left of the target, we tend to assume one of two things: either the player has turned insufficiently or the back of the left hand is forced over the shaft, producing a laid-off position.

FAR LEFT: A danger is of trying to point the club on line at the top of the backswing. It depends on the degree of shoulder turn and is achieved by turning, not lifting. If short, like Nick Price's , it doesn't come round on target

LEFT: John Daly's long backswing goes beyond the line!

Certainly there are some golfing faults where the top of the backswing simply isn't aimed correctly and the player is likely to produce an inconsistent attack. If he turns insufficiently in the backswing and aims the club left of target, he may well become right-side dominant in the downswing with an out-to-in, cutter's action. Increasing the turn of the left side and working at getting the club on target may pay dividends. We may see a player whose club shaft points way right of target because the right hand is up

Making the backswing simple – coiling from the feet and knees, the wrists cocking when they feel ready to do so, clubface parallel to the left arm from a good grip and left side in control

Bernhard Langer in a tightly coiled position, backside out, right leg stable, knees flexed and the shoulders turning against the resistance of the feet and knees

behind the shaft rather than beneath it. This may well encourage some bad delivery position and contact.

But the fallacy is to *try* to point the club in the right direction as though this is the be all and end all of a good backswing. Firstly, the club will point round in the correct direction only at a certain length. The swing is essentially a rounded movement with the club moving round behind the player. If his swing is short, the club may not reach the point where it comes round to point on target. If on the other hand it is long and goes beyond the horizontal, it will inevitably find a position where it points right of our parallel line.

The greatest danger seems to be with the short swinger or the tall golfer who doesn't quite reach the horizontal in the backswing – indeed, why should he? Over-emphasis on pointing the club in the right direction leads many players to take the club back into a takeaway position where the club hardly gets level with the body or legs, and then from there to hitch it directly upwards with a feeling early in the backswing of pointing the club 'on target'. (I use this phrase 'on target' but it is of course parallel to the target line.) The player begins to take the club back and then to lift it too directly without letting the club come round and back behind him. This results in the wrists cocking upwards instead of backwards and encourages the player to come down in an unsatisfactory early hit position.

Many students of the game misinterpret what they see and hear. A common misconception is to find a halfway-back, hip-height position and then to take the club straight up from there in the search to point the club on line. Nick Faldo's 'waggle' – setting the club parallel to the ground and to the shot – led golfers to believe that this should be followed by lifting the arms and club straight up to point it on target. In reality his feeling was of cocking the wrists and finding this position, from there *turning the shoulders* to bring the club round on target. A very different story.

4 MORE BACKSWING THOUGHTS

KEEPING THE HEAD STILL

Medium- and high-handicap golfers often suffer through an obsession with keeping the head still, particularly on the backswing. On occasions top-class golfers fall into the same trap.

On the backswing, the head must move a touch to enable the shoulders to turn fully. To demonstrate this, hold a club across your shoulders and behind your head, grip to the left. Focus your eyes on a spot on the wall or a mirror straight in front of you and turn your shoulders fully until the end of the club points directly opposite you to the spot. To achieve this full

In the backswing the head must turn just a touch, shoulder slightly covering the chin, the left eye looking at the ball and the view of the right eye possibly slightly restricted. The eyes are then firmly focused on the ball through impact (Ben Crenshaw)

shoulder turn, the head has to move fractionally, your nose moving perhaps half an inch or so.

The same has to happen on the backswing. The head cannot stay absolutely still with the shoulders making their correct turn. The player with insufficient shoulder turn and a laid off position at the top of the backswing is sometimes too still with the head to allow the turn to take place.

Correctly, by the top of the backswing the head will have turned slightly and your right eye, instead of looking at the ball, now looks at the side of your nose. Hence the theory of looking at the back of the ball with your left eye. The problem can be more acute for the player who is definitely right-eye dominant and resists the feeling of letting the left eye do the work.

Although 'head still' can be exaggerated in the backswing, watching the ball does apply. Frequently at the end of a purple patch, when things just start to deteriorate, it is all too easy to find oneself not watching the ball quite long enough through impact. See the ball, the grass and then look up. But give the head its necessary freedom in the backswing.

The other 'head still' problem can arise if the player gets the wrong relationship between the chin and the shoulders. In the backswing the left shoulder should slightly cover the chin. In the throughswing the right shoulder should again slightly cover it. The chin should be in rather than out. Some players, particularly those with fairly narrow shoulders, let the left shoulder get under the chin on the backswing – i.e. between the chin and the chest – and then do the same in the throughswing. The arms tend to be forced into a flattish plane on both backswing and throughswing, with the head feeling as if it is forced up through impact. The best cure is to practise swinging (definitely without a ball) with the mouth slightly open. This lowers the player's jaw and gives a definite feeling of the shoulders moving against the chin rather than between chin and chest.

THE PLANE AND YOUR VIEW OF THE BALL – BALL POSITION

One of the most difficult backswing faults to correct is that of the player who tips his shoulders in the backswing, dropping the left shoulder into a steep, upright plane. There are high swings and steep swings. Tom Watson, for example, turns his shoulders on a fairly horizontal plane yet lifts his arms. The lift is made with the arm movement and not the shoulders dropping or tipping. Club golfers, instead of just lifting the arms, will often make the up, down, up movement with the shoulders. The steep shoulder tip tends to produce a steep attack into the ball. This may work well with the shorter irons but produces insufficient roundness to achieve sound direction and good penetration with the longer clubs and driver.

Correcting the plane of the shoulder turn can often be difficult. With this steep shoulder tip the player feels in control and able to get back down to the ball again. Flatten the plane of backswing and the player will invariably start topping the ball, feeling great awkwardness at getting back to it at all.

To correct the shoulder plane, let's first see why it happens. The fault is often one of playing the ball well opposite his left foot too early in his career. He simply cannot turn his shoulders on a fairly horizontal plane and still comfortably see the ball. He begins to drop the left shoulder in an attempt to see the ball clearly and peers at it in the hope of making a good contact. He wants to see it with both eyes, and he wants to see as much of it as possible. Correctly, when we look at a ball at address we look at the back of the ball (or back inside of the ball). As we turn in the backswing the left shoulder moves as if threatening to hide the ball. The more horizontal the shoulder turn, the more uncomfortable the view of the ball. By the top of the backswing, the head turns fractionally and your left eye looks at the back of the ball and your right at your nose and your shoulder. But the newer golfer often doesn't like the feeling of the left shoulder coming up into view. He wants to see the whole ball and will often see all the ground between the ball and his feet. If faced with a player with a steep swing I usually ask whether he can see his feet at the top of the backswing. He glows with pride and tells me he can. But for all but the very tallest of golfers the feet should never come into view.

So a starting point in correcting the plane of the swing, whether with a high-handicap or an advanced player, is to think about the view of the ball. If the ball is moved back in the stance a touch, to a point 3 or 4 inches inside the left heel, it becomes easier to make a more confident turn away from it and to resist the feeling of dropping the left shoulder and peering at the ball. That is the first stage. As an exercise, put down three pegs between the ball and the feet at, say, 4-inch intervals. At the top of the backswing check how much ground you see. Ideally see the ball and the first tee but not the second or the third, and certainly not the feet. For the higher-handicap player it is also a question of encouraging him to see the ball with the left eye and not to expect to see it with the right.

The feeling in trying to flatten the plane is of trying to lift the left shoulder in the backswing, as though trying to hide the ball. The arms can lift as necessary. From the top of the backswing the feeling is of swinging *under* the left shoulder and up into the finish.

This is a difficult error to correct, but once the visual problem is understood it can be tackled in a more understanding and meaningful way.

ARM PLANE AND SHOULDER PLANE

At the top of the backswing the plane of the arm movement should always be above the shoulder turn. In other words, the shoulders should turn fairly horizontally while the left arm lifts slightly above this angle. To some players the left arm and shoulder plane stay very much together. To others, the left arm is certainly lifted above the shoulders.

What must not happen is for the shoulders to tip and the arms to move under that plane. It is a problem that is usually associated with players who shut the clubface early in the backswing, never reaching a backswing where the club is supported on the left thumb. The player often allows the left arm to move under the shoulders, right elbow moving out behind him in the takeaway instead of folding in and under. It is a common fault of golfing hockey players. The player who takes the club away with a low left-arm position, often cramping the right elbow outwards behind him, usually finds it impossible to make any wrist-cock and to get the club sitting up on the left thumb. The wrists work against themselves, tending to hinge backwards, and the backswing becomes short and restricted.

The key correction is to ensure that the right elbow seems to stay sitting against the right hip and to stay relatively still in the takeaway. The right arm pivots from that point, elbow forward, not out behind. The player can now get the feeling of turning away and getting the right hand more beneath the club with the left arm lifting into the correct plane.

The correct feeling in the backswing is of separating the arms and shoulders, left arm swinging slightly higher than the shoulder plane. This means that the arms and shoulders have begun to work independently of each other. The left arm needs its freedom to enable it to work away from the right shoulder in the downswing. If, by contrast, the left arm works below the shoulders, the two tend to stick together. The right shoulder then tends to push from the top instead of the left arm being able to work away freely.

Sometimes the feeling needs to be that of the right shoulder and right side staying subservient in the backswing, in the slightly crumpled, low position in which they started. From here the feeling can be of lifting the arms into a higher plane than the shoulders. Wrongly, if the right side stretches the right shoulder works up. In turn the shoulder plane tends to steepen and arms and shoulders lose their separation.

The player with too steep a shoulder plane often tries to look too intently at the ball and sees his feet at the top of the backswing. In this exercise pegs are set from feet to ball. The player learns to turn the left shoulder more horizontally until he sees the ball and first peg but never the feet

KEYS FOR FLAT SWINGERS

The more common fault with the plane of the swing, is one of producing a high, steep swing rather than of producing too flat a plane. The instinctive way for most people to strike a ball which sits on the ground is to pick up the club and chop it down, easily making contact with the ball without the ground getting in the way. Most novices attacking a golf ball are unlikely to swing the club in too flat a plane, because the flatter the plane, the more the ground tends to get in the way of the contact. Those who start as children are usually encouraged to set the ball opposite the middle of the feet and from here to turn. A flatter plane of swing is certainly much easier for someone fairly small and far easier than with the ball out towards the left heel. But relatively speaking, a swing which is too flat is fairly uncommon.

The plane of the swing should, in the broadest terms and for the simplest possible swing, simply follow the angle of the club shaft at address. The merits of a flattish plane mean that the player is unlikely to become dominant with the right side, producing the steep, out-to-in swing which besets the majority of club players.

But certainly, to some, a flat plane of swing can cause problems. For the longer handicap player it may be through complete dominance with the right hand, with the left hand and thumb giving no control at the top of the backswing. The left arm simply drops, particularly with tiredness, allowing the backswing to flatten. The other flat plane action, again often found among club golfers, is where the body lifts and the hip angle straightens and is lost in the backswing. The legs really do stay lifeless and the left shoulder gets too high. It may even occasionally hide the view of the ball.

Barry Lane's flat backswing will inevitably produce a powerful inside attack. All the power is directed forwards, not downwards. The drawback of a flat backswing can be less height at times than may be needed

For the advanced golfer who has a flat swing, however, there needs to be a degree of caution before trying to change it. Is the flat swing actually causing problems or is it in fact the sort of action most top-class, tall golfers like Nick Faldo would give anything for? The great thing with a flattish plane of swing is that the good golfer will invariably attack the ball from the inside and with a shallow attack. The drawback, perhaps, is that the player might find difficulty in getting height to shots and may be hampered by inadequate carry in some situations. Lee Trevino once vowed never to play again at Augusta in the Masters because he didn't enjoy the course. It was put down to the fact that his flat swing didn't flight the ball high enough. His love affair with the course, I presume, was rekindled on a better day!

The player who is concerned about a flat plane needs to understand how this usually occurs. It does not generally occur through the player taking the club in a shallow takeaway and then continuing round on this plane. Far more likely is that the player takes the club back on a fairly straightish and if anything upright takeaway and then allows the left arm to move up and over into a flattish position. Imagine a big-busted lady having to lift her left arm to clear her bosom and then allowing it to move over into a flattish position! That's how the flat swing happens. The more the player is encouraged to take the club back straight and high, the less able he is to produce height in the backswing. The opposite, in fact, is often the cure. The wrists should be lowered at address, taking the club far more on the inside and into a toe-up position at hip-height. From here, the arms can lift. The swing needs to be seen as a turn and then a lift. The flattish swinger may get into his position by making a lift and then a turn. Frequently this style of player allows the club to move several inches off the ground in the takeaway.

As an exercise put a tee peg 18 inches behind the ball and perhaps 4 inches inside the line and try to knock it over in the backswing. This gives the feeling of turning more inside and encouraging the arms to lift.

The feeling for the flat swinger trying to raise the plane of the swing is therefore often the precise opposite of what he imagines – a turn followed by a lift rather than vice versa.

The flat backswing is often produced by lifting and then turning, like Lee Trevino. Picking the club up higher in the takeaway can exaggerate the feeling. The correction, if desired, is to turn **and then** lift

ON STARTING BACK

The backswing has to start in a well-timed, coordinated manner. One theory is that there should hardly be a stationary position but always a feeling of fluidity. The argument is that this never allows the player to become static at address, thus minimising difficulties in the takeaway. Possibly the danger for some is that it is too imprecise.

The key point for the takeaway is to ensure that you fully support the club at address. From here we all have some little trigger movement which starts us into action. The most common among professionals is a little kick forward and left with the right knee before pushing back smoothly. The trigger for Jack Nicklaus is the head just turning away a touch. For Lee Trevino it is a small, but ever constant, movement with the left toes. Others show the tiniest forward press in the hands which, providing the movement is minuscule, possibly causes no difficulties.

But the danger of the forward press is that the grip can be allowed to move. The left hand may tighten and turn over a touch, the right may slide under. It may work on the practice ground but then be exaggerated under pressure. A shifting grip is rarely corrected unless replaced with another movement to act as the trigger. Far safer is the little kick of the right knee. Another fault emerging under pressure is excess tension, displaying itself in a little lift of the shoulders. This again acts as the player's 'Ready, steady, go' movement, often associated with changes in the breathing pattern at anxious moments. Any unwanted tension of the shoulders needs to be directed downwards, never upwards.

Ideally, the backswing is made in the address position and the takeaway, with as little thought as possible after the club has moved back 18 inches or so. Certainly on the golf course the rest of the backswing must freewheel itself into action from here, with the brain firmly working forwards to the target. Thoughts of the takeaway are associated largely with the direction of swing and the desired attack on the ball. The desired shallow attack of the driver requires a shallow takeaway. The feeling of an inside attack requires an inside takeaway.

If we return to our concept of a hammer striking a nail sideways, the takeaway is a rehearsal of the attack.

TAKE AN AXE TO A TREE TO FEEL YOUR SWING

Good golfers, as a rule, turn the top half of the body in the backswing and produce a shallow attack on the ball, while club golfers tend to pick the club up and produce a steep attack. The problem, of course, is that we are trying to hit a very small ball which sits on the ground and the ground gets in the way. A turning movement and a shallow attack initially feel far more difficult than a downward chopping movement.

My analogy is to explain that the professional golfer with an axe in his hand looks as though he his trying to chop down a tree standing out some-

The key to a good backswing is to rehearse the hitting position at address, to feel an attack from **behind** oneself and to keep the brain firmly moving **forward** throughout

where opposite his left foot. He turns the top half of his body and would take a hefty sideways swing at the tree.

The typical long handicap golfer, by contrast, looks as though the professional golfer has felled the tree for him; it is now lying on the ground and his idea is to chop up and down as though hewing it into logs!

For the low-handicap golfer, particularly one finding a shallow attack with the driver a problem, this concept can sometimes help to explain how the top half of the body correctly turns and coils against the legs – as it would with an axe – with the feeling of maximum power in the delivery back to impact.

Much the same is felt moving into a position from which to throw a ball or javelin at full stretch. The legs stay in position, providing stability and resistance, while the top half coils. The thought of an axe felling a tree emphasises the width and attempt at a relatively horizontal attack, with power being generated in a sideways direction. For this reason, a shortish player, swinging on a neutral or flattish plane, will often generate as much or more power than a taller player, whose swing is inevitably more upright, with potential power ready to be released downwards rather than forwards.

IS YOUR BACKSWING LIKE A FINGERPRINT?

Let's go back to the basic principle of becoming a better golfer. Remember that there are two routes. Are we trying to make our best swing as repetitive as possible or are we trying to change our best swing?

I often question whether it really is possible to change a player's backswing dramatically. Sandy Lyle spent much time and money trying to alter a backswing he didn't like. Nick Faldo once joked to me that he had been to Sandy's birthday party and had given him a Nick Faldo instructional tape, and that it was then that the rot set in! I don't think for one moment it was true, but perhaps Nick's quest to rebuild his swing, with such obvious success, led Sandy to dabble with the same thoughts. Sandy, however, was unable to change. He may look back at videos of his swing before the slump occurred and after his form revived and point to some difference, but in fact there probably is none. And yet no doubt he worked for hour upon hour practising different and complex movements. Possibly they weren't changes at all, just new sensations. Fortunately he apparently abandoned most of the advice he was given and returned to the simple methods of his father's teaching, developed early in childhood.

The best advice in such circumstances? Simply to stand on the practice ground, trust the backswing he had always made and concentrate on ball control, delivering the clubface to the ball correctly and hitting the ball where he wanted. Sure, most players would like to have a backswing like

Ernie Els showing a powerful coiling in the backswing, shoulders turning against the resistance of the legs and hips. From here everything moves through at speed to a full, controlled, balanced finish – the position club golfers rarely learn to achieve

Hogan's. Some do and some don't. Of course there are players whose backswings need work. But if Sandy were to have a perfect backswing it would have been firmly established by the age of 12, not in his thirties. At an advanced level the backswing is often like a fingerprint and it simply cannot be changed. Indeed, it should not be tampered with unnecessarily.

Undoubtedly we can change the first couple of feet of the takeaway thereby altering the direction or plane; but from there, the swing has to freewheel to the top of the backswing. If the mind is working backwards to control the backswing it can rarely think forwards sufficiently to control the important delivery into impact.

If the backswing feels wrong, search first for the correct feeling at address. Next, rehearse your delivery on the ball and let that guide you back. Thirdly, perhaps think of the takeaway to set it all in the right direction. But as a general rule, leave well alone unless you really are sure that the work will pay dividends. Is the change necessary? Has the swing changed or does it just feel different as a result of concentrating your thoughts on part of your body or swing you usually ignore?

5

CHANGING DIRECTIONS – THROUGH THE BALL

TURN AND RETURN

In the simplest form of swing, the impact is rehearsed mentally and physically at address. The swing moves back away from the ball and returns in an identical (or seemingly identical) path to the same position, strikes the ball and then follows on through. The club and swing move on a constant plane, determined by the club shaft at address. Backswing, downswing and follow-through all match.

In the simplest of swings address and impact are virtually identical (hips just through a touch more in the strike) with takeaway and attack following the same path

An excellent way of feeling this is to set up and have a few whacks at an old car tyre. I don't particularly like this as a strengthening exercise; it tends to produce a deceleration into the ball. But use it to feel the symmetry of backswing and downswing. Feel an address position. Turn off this and return to it, striking the tyre solidly. Back and through. It gives the feeling of the relationship of address and impact, the takeaway and attack. Any loop or movement off plane in the swing begins to be felt. Impact feels different from address. And yet it shouldn't. Very often the feeling of impact is of the shoulders and hips being too active and ahead. The exercise emphasises the need to return the arms and club to their starting point in time with the body.

Now move away from the tyre and make the same feeling of backswing and downswing but then moving into the follow-through. Feel address, swing back, return to address, hesitate a moment and then finish the swing. Turn, return and bring the movements to the simplest form possible.

Moving back and through, back and through to strike a tyre soon shows if the address position and hitting position don't match. Emphasis usually needs to be put on returning the club and arms early enough, and on the same path as the takeaway, before the hips and legs get too active

TURN AND LIFT – DOWN AND TURN

Swinging the club back is basically a question of turning the body and then lifting the arms. To some this feels like two distinct movements. Ultimately, of course, it should blend into one simple one. But the two elements are there.

The difficulty for most people is putting the whole action smoothly into reverse. In the backswing the movement is one of turning the body and the arms then lifting. To move into reverse correctly the arms should now drop down and the body turn on through. The problem for nearly all golfers is that instead of the arms dropping down, followed by a turn of the body, the easier and wrong movement is for the right side of the body to start turning first before the arms start their downward movement. This invariably brings the club down in too steep an attack, for the longer-handicap player usually cutting across the line of the shot.

For many top-class golfers the feeling of putting everything into reverse is almost one of the body staying still fractionally at the top of the backswing while both arms are lowered or dropped behind from the top of the back-swing to enable the attack to be shallower. In some players this is quite noticeable. Nick Price has a distinctive movement of settling the arms down behind himself to change directions. So, very clearly do Nick Faldo and Fred Couples. Ben Hogan had the same movement. So how does one achieve it?

There are two ideas to try depending on your feeling of the turn in the backswing. If the feeling is one of making a tight turn, legs seeming to stay fairly still and the shoulders turning, the correct sensation from there is one of keeping the whole upper body still for a fraction of a second and literally lowering both arms down behind you. Remember that this may not actu-

To set the swing into reverse the arms start their move down before the body turns through too early. Turn and left, down and turn – a movement very visible with both Nick Price and Nick Faldo

ally happen, and probably does not need to happen but what it does do is to stop the right side taking over prematurely. From there the delivery can be from behind the player, right wrist still set back on itself and with a feeling of being able to attack the ball with a shallow path. The sensation for the very good player may be one of holding back on the right foot for longer, almost feeling that the foot will stay flat on the ground into impact. The heel will unquestionably begin to be pulled off the ground but by sitting back on the right side longer it again gives the feeling of the arms starting the movement down before the right side unwinds. The advice of trying to stay on the right foot longer into impact applies only to the *very* good player. The danger for the medium- or higher-handicap player is that by immobilising the legs a touch the top half becomes even more dominant. It is an exercise only for the good golfer.

The other feeling, of bringing the arms down before the body turns, is more applicable to the player with a slightly fuller, looser turn. Here there is a sense of turning into the top of the backswing, holding the turn and then almost trying to get the arms and club back to impact before the body returns to its address position and is ultimately pulled on through. The feeling is of turning the shoulders, staying turned and hitting with the arms, the direction of attack feeling to be along the line of the hips. All the time we are trying to discourage the right shoulder and right side from unwinding.

The feeling of timing, particularly with a driver can be crucial. The harder the player tries to hit the ball the more dominant the right side can become. The timing, particularly for those prone to fading or slicing under pressure is rather like four-horse race. Having swung the club round to the top of the backswing there are four contestants fighting to win the race back round to impact – the clubhead, the hands, the hips and the right shoulder. The hips have but a few inches to travel and always start as firm favourite. The right shoulder has a little further to make up and is the strongest and most aggressive. The hands have rather further to travel but are susceptible to the pressure of the occasion. But the clubhead has by far the longest journey and, for many, very little chance of coming in the winner. In reality the hips should and will always win the race. But the other three should all arrive together.

If the shoulders or hands lead, the clubface is invariably left open for a fade or slice. For those who do tend to fade or slice the feeling must be of making the clubhead win. But it has to travel in a rounded direction and can't take a short cut down and across the race track! The more the feeling of trying to generate power, the harder the right shoulder tends to work and the less chance of all three reaching the finishing line together. The feeling needs to be one of curbing the thrust of the shoulders and waiting for the clubhead to come round from behind you to catch the others, swinging the left arm away from the right shoulder to give the clubhead a chance. If, as unusually happens, the clubhead wins and the shoulders or hands (or indeed the hips) lag behind, the result is a hook.

LEFT SIDE TO RIGHT – LEFT AWAY FROM RIGHT

A good feeling in the backswing is of the right side staying fairly still and the left side moving to it. The shoulders round in, left one closing towards right one. The left arm moves across towards the right shoulder and slightly up; the left knee moves in towards the right leg, even if we try to resist this movement. Once we get to the top of the backswing we want the right side to be relatively subservient and for the left one to move away from it. Key movements for many players are usually associated with this. Even those who insist that the shot is made in the backswing acknowledge that the most important thought can be of separating the left side away from the right to start the downswing, rather than the right side pushing.

At the top of the backswing the right shoulder tends to be in a dominant position. The easy but wrong feeling of generating power into the shot is for the

In the backswing the left arm swings to the right shoulder. The right shoulder then stays passive while the left arm moves down and away from it.

right shoulder to thrust forward. For most golfers it is a constant battle to keep the right side in a passive role.

Correctly, from the top of the backswing the space between the left arm and the right shoulder should immediately widen as the downswing starts. The feeling should be of swinging the left arm to the right shoulder in the backswing and then of swinging it away from the right shoulder. The danger is of sticking the left arm to the right shoulder and the right shoulder then pushing it down again.

The more the left arm can be in control of the backswing and the start of the downswing the better. If you take a club in your left hand only, the feeling should be of swinging the left arm up towards the right shoulder and then swinging it away again. This is fine. Put the right hand on the club as well and the whole movement may feel more difficult.

A useful feeling is that of symmetry through the swing, the left arm and club swinging to the right shoulder and the right arm and club then swinging towards the left shoulder. Although in some ways this begins to put emphasis on the right hand and arm perhaps a little too early, it does mean

To discourage the right shoulder from putting in unwanted power the feeling is of the left arm swinging to the right shoulder in the backswing, the arms then swinging past the body to the left shoulder

that the left arm very definitely moves the club away from the right shoulder rather than allowing the right shoulder to push. As an exercise swing the club back, thinking of the left arm going to the right shoulder; the right arm naturally folds away. Then reverse the movement and think of the right arm moving to the left shoulder and the left arm folding away. It produces a feeling of the arms swinging away and across the body, leaving the legs and shoulders less active. The shallower attack, emphasising the arm action and keeping the upper body passive, may give the feeling of sitting back on the heels more through the imaginary impact zone.

The related leg action for many tournament pros is of thrusting back into the left heel, moving the left knee away from the right one, clearing with the left side and moving the left hip out of the way. They are all movements which presuppose that the left side has moved towards the right in the backswing as though closing onto it, then being free to open up and move away from it as everything moves into reverse. Again, the more left-side control the right-handed player can encourage the better this movement is likely to be.

LEG ACTION – TOE, HEEL FOR POWER

The leg action feels as though the left side is dragged round towards the right in the backswing. The left knee and leg then pulls and opens away from the right – hence the widening of the knees – the right leg eventually being pulled on through after impact

Some professionals are adamant that the left heel should never lift in the backswing. Sam Snead, for one, believed it was entirely incorrect. On the other hand, Jack Nicklaus and Tom Watson both pick the heel up high. I don't like to see advanced golfers lifting the heel if they can help it, but striving to keep the heel on the ground unnaturally can cause problems.

For a good, powerful leg action the knees are knocked slightly inwards, with a sensation of strength and spring. In the backswing the weight simply moves round and forward onto the ball of the left foot, back slightly on the right heel but with the right knee remaining strong and flexed. Let's ignore whether or not the left heel actually lifts. By having the knees knocked in at address, the left knee automatically points diagonally inwards as though pointing towards the ball. Don't force it; it happens. In the downswing the correct movement is then to push the weight backwards towards the left heel, left knee and left hip pulling backwards and the left leg then twisting in the down- and throughswing to bring the hips round on target. It is a forward and backward movement, onto the ball of the foot and then back towards the heel.

The player who lifts the left heel should correctly keep all the toes of the left foot on the ground. The foot definitely bends and folds. The little toe is still in contact with the ground. There should be no moving in onto the inside of the big toe or the turn becomes loose instead of producing a tight, coiled turn. If the heel does lift it must be a steady, gradual lift and not a sudden release of tension.

The danger in forcing the left heel to stay down is of rolling onto the inside of the foot. If you roll on the inside of the foot in the backswing you roll onto the outside in the throughswing, letting the left leg bow out to the side with too much lateral hip movement. It is unlikely that the legs and hips will turn through correctly towards the target if there is a lateral rolling on the backswing. Ideally in the throughswing the balance is poised on the back two thirds of the left foot – you should be able to wiggle the toes of the left foot – without a feeling of rolling onto the outside of it.

Occasionally we see players who swing to the top of the backswing, keep the left heel on the ground and allow too much weight to hang over the left foot. The feeling in getting the top half behind the ball must still be that there is a direct push down into the ball of the left foot. The whole coiling of the backswing starts from there. The pressure and push in the left foot are diagonally downwards but must always be done with the whole of the ball of the foot still remaining on the ground. With the weight distribution moving forward onto the ball of the foot and back on the heel, the left leg can move correctly. The left knee, unless moving too freely, will invariably find the correct position in the backswing. From here the leg can be drawn out of the way for good clearance in the throughswing.

BALL POSITION AND LEG ACTION

Positioning the ball too far forward towards the left foot usually causes poor leg action and appears to cause back problems. The correct feeling of the leg action from the top of the backswing is for the left hip and left leg to pull directly behind the player. An excellent exercise is to stand beside a wall, outside of the left foot jammed against it and feet apart as though in an address position. With your hands in your trouser pockets simulate the feeling of the backswing turn and then move the body and legs through into a follow-through position. The left leg should be able to clear round away from the wall without moving out towards it.

This movement can be difficult. There may be insufficient flexibility in the ankle and knee to allow the left leg to pull back and be reasonably straight at the end of the swing, hips turned through.

Once this feeling is put into the good golfer's swing, there is always enough lateral movement to the left in the downswing. The longer-handicap could leave himself back on the right foot. But the good player will always move onto the left leg and make a lateral hip and leg movement. What he doesn't necessarily do is to thrust back correctly onto the left heel and to get the leg out of the way.

If the player positions the ball too far towards the left heel it becomes difficult to turn the legs and hips out of the way and the player is constantly struggling to find the bottom of the ball. The hips and legs tend to shift to the left, left hip rising and right hip dropping, and firmness at the end of the swing tends to be lost.

The old-fashioned idea of 'hitting against a firm left side' was a good one. The left leg needn't be rigid at the end of the swing but it should be balanced and as far as possible reasonably straight, though not locked. The tall golfer with a short iron usually has difficulty in finding space for the left leg, but the golfer of 6 foot or less should be able to move through into a stable left leg position. The further forward the ball is played, the more difficult the leg action can become. Instead of simply using the legs as a firm base for the swing, turning and then turning back on the left leg, the feeling becomes one of sliding the legs and kicking with the right knee in an attempt to meet the ball from a slightly awkward position.

Swings that last well into middle age, without causing back problems, seem to be those where the left leg works steadily and firmly. Players such

With the left foot against a wall, hands in the pockets, practise thrusting back towards the left heel, hip and leg pulling directly backwards rather than shifting sideways into the wall. At speed in the swing the good golfer will always get enough lateral movement towards the target but this creates the right feeling

The tall golfer needs to stand up well, giving space for the left leg to work correctly through impact. In the backswing the weight moves round and forward onto the ball of the left foot. In the throughswing the weight moves backwards into the left heel, left leg and hip pulling back into a stable position, leg straight though not locked

as Jack Nicklaus, Bernhard Langer and Seve Ballesteros, who show a lot of bowing of the left leg, seem to encounter back problems, almost certainly twisting the spine at great speed and great pressure.

INSIDE EQUALS SHALLOW, OUTSIDE EQUALS STEEP

Most world-class golfers like to attack the ball with a relatively shallow attack. If you strike the ball with an inside attack it will be shallow. If you strike the ball with a shallow attack it will be from the inside. Conversely, if you strike the ball from out-to-in or from straight down the line it will be steep, and if steep it is likely to be out-to-in.

The reason why most players initially find it hard to make an inside attack is that it is also shallow. The ground tends to get in the way of a shallow attack far more than it does the steep attack. Even players of a very low handicap are often troubled by a feeling of hitting slightly across the ball or being unable to attack the ball from as far inside as they would like.

Very often the player can improve the direction of the strike simply by working on the concept of a shallower attack. If he feels that the ball is being swept cleanly from the top of the grass, rather than allowing himself to take a divot, this is likely to go hand in hand with a more inside strike. The great Tommy Armour always insisted on teaching his pupils from a low tee peg. I believe one of the aims of this was to encourage the player to pick the ball off a little more cleanly, to discourage a feeling of digging and to enable the player to contact the ball from the inside. A feeling of sweeping the ball up and away from a low tee produces an inside attack far more easily than placing the ball on a poor or tight lie.

Obviously we can't play all our golf with the ball teed up or sitting on a good lie. But to correct a slightly steep out-to-in attack, practise from a perfect lie to encourage a shallow contact and then learn to reproduce that same feeling with the ball sitting less well.

On a driving range mat, work at almost grazing the ground on an inside curve just before striking the ball. The closer the clubhead stays to the ground before impact, without actually contacting it, the more inside the attack is likely to be. Although slightly exaggerated this gives the feeling of meeting the ball correctly.

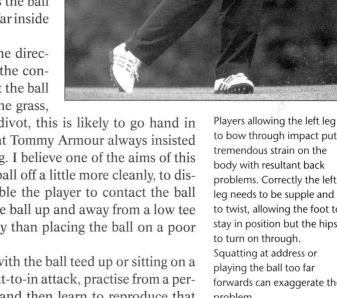

Players allowing the left leg to bow through impact put tremendous strain on the body with resultant back problems. Correctly the left leg needs to be supple and to twist, allowing the foot to stay in position but the hips to turn on through. Squatting at address or playing the ball too far forwards can exaggerate the problem

Many golfers set up to the ball in one position and strike it with the hands in a much higher position through impact. The downswing, in turn, is considerably steeper than the backswing. The hands will almost always move upwards slightly between address and impact – the very speed of the action I suspect throwing arms and club into a straight line – but for many players this higher hand position is a giveaway of something going wrong in the downswing. Trying to repeat the hand position of address at impact is difficult to feel with the ball but is certainly something to work at in practice. Feel that address is a forward-thinking rehearsal of impact – as though posing for a still photo of the contact. The hips will almost certainly have turned through more, but the feeling should be that the hands and arms return on the same plane and same direction of attack as they went back on.

To many club golfers, the hardest part of the swing is being able to strike the ball from the inside. Remember that the aim is not to hit from in-to-out in a straight line; this produces a push. The feeling through impact must be of a curved path. The club attacks the ball from the inside, is directed on target at the moment of impact, and then returns on a smooth, symmetrical curve beyond impact. But it is the approach to impact which causes the problems. Firstly, if an outside attack is the fault, check the ball position. Be prepared to pull the ball back in the stance. Think first of the direction of the clubhead into impact.

Ian Woosnam with a shallow, inside attack. The feeling is often one of holding back the right side, giving the hands room to return to impact from the inside. If, by contrast, the right hip is too active the hands and hip can fight, producing a steeper or outside attack

On a driving range mat, put some light obstacle, say, 18 inches behind the ball and fractionally outside it – a Coke can (empty) is ideal. Concentrate on getting the clubhead away inside this, and attacking it from inside. Many a club golfer hits the can or even comes down over the top of it. Don't worry how you achieve the direction of the strike. Think most of the clubhead and forget your body. If this doesn't work, check the degree of turn in the backswing. Feel that the shoulders turn, stay turned and give you time to get the clubhead back to the ball before the right side works in prematurely. Turn and hit along the hips. Frequently, emphasis on moving the hips and legs too early in the downswing puts the right hip forward into a position where it is in the way of an inside attack. Try the tyre exercise. Feel address. Return to it on impact. Have the legs, hips and shoulders got ahead? Emphasise returning the arms and club to the tyre early enough, feeling the same posture as address, backside out with room for the inside attack.

Remember that the feeling of the attack is like striking a nail sideways with a hammer. The backward and forward movements should follow the same path. Working at ensuring the club moves away on the inside can help. Sometimes, however, a takeaway which is too much inside encourages an outside loop on the downswing. The feeling may at times need to be of taking the club a little straighter back and working on the feeling of an inside loop. In fact the club probably doesn't describe an inside loop (though if it did it wouldn't matter). The feeling of the inside loop is probably simply eradicating the outside loop and beginning to bring the club on its correct inside, shallow path. Work primarily at feeling the path of the clubhead and let your body move in sympathy with this. Don't get over-concerned with body movements.

So, if troubled by a slightly out-to-in swing, aim at producing a slightly shallower attack; focus on that and it may well pay dividends.

TALL PLAYERS – WHERE DOES THE BEND GO?

The difficulty for the tall golfer is that inevitably he has to bend more from the hips at address, and stands closer to the ball with the legs well flexed. The smaller golfer bending from the hips and keeping the legs relaxed shows hardly any knee flex. The tall golfer bending over more will automatically balance himself differently. The problem for the tall golfer is that he usually returns to impact with the knees still bent. The difficulty is what happens from there on through.

Set up at address, conscious that this is preparation for impact, swing to the top of the backswing and return to impact, feeling a virtual repetition of address. That's fine. But what happens now? If the left leg is bent it has nowhere to go. If the tall golfer correctly returns to impact with the same posture and hip angle as address, the question is where the bend goes from there. There are three options.

For the tall golfer the bend in the hips must be retained on the backswing and through to impact. From there one type of swing simply allows the bend to be released, moving on through and up into a majestic finish just after impact. Timing of the upward release, particularly with a short iron, is crucial

A second way of getting rid of the bend is for the bend in the hips to be translated into a twisting under through impact, often associated with a fader's action and shots cutting away to the right under pressure

The first is for the player to return to impact, watch the ball well, then allow himself to stand up taller and produce a majestic finish. The left leg will be fairly straight and the head considerably higher than it was at address. Ballesteros, though not particularly tall, produces this sort of movement where there is a definite change of level in the swing. He swings back, returns to impact and then moves on through and very definitely up. In other words, the bend in the hips at address has been repeated through impact and the bend then straightens up into the finish.

The second way in which the tall player can swing is for that bend in the hips to become a twisting under of the top half through impact. We see this position with Greg Norman and many other tall golfers. The player starts with a bend from the hips. The more he bends over at address the more the upper body twists under as he returns to impact, and by the end of the swing he may produce a position where the right shoulder seems to stay very low. Technically the danger here is that the hips begin to tilt and tip and the swing may tend to get too steep. The bend at address becomes a twisting under of the right side, possibly throwing the left hip and leg out a touch beyond impact and if anything with a tendency to block shots high and away to the right.

The third type of movement corresponds very much with what happens in the backswing. The taller the player, the more the bend from the hips at address. As he turns his upper body in the backswing, this bend from the hips automatically sees the head and shoulders move more behind the ball than for a smaller player. In returning to impact in the same way the hip bend is retained in the throughswing. In other words, instead of twisting under or releasing the bend and standing up, it is as though the top half is allowed to move on through with the head travelling several inches beyond impact. In other words, the hip angle stays constant not just in the backswing but in the throughswing. The tall player who adopts this type of movement is able to produce a flatter plane of swing both back and through rather than twisting or straightening up.

To feel a very exaggerated version of this movement, set up in your address position without a golf ball and bend right over as though touching your toes. Turn to the right and your head automatically turns round to the right; then turn round to the left. Now stand up straighter, approaching the posture of your address position; once again turn to your right and now turn to the left. The bend in the hips remains constant. Now in a more erect position, just as at address, allow the same movement to take place. Put your hands at the top of your legs, feeling the bend in the hips and feeling that the bend stays constant.

My own impression of Nick Faldo's swing is that under David Leadbetter's guidance he moved from the second type of swing – right shoulder twisting underneath, hips if anything tilting – to the third kind of swing. Instead of the bend being released or becoming a twist, it is as though the bend in the hips stays through impact far longer and for this reason the head moves noticeably left of the ball through impact. The shoulders simply turn and turn instead of being forced underneath.

The third option for the tall golfer is for the bend in the hips to be retained well beyond impact. This shows the upper body moving on through and ahead after impact – the inherent danger being for the right side to come over the top for shots dragged away to the left

So for the tall golfer, in answer to the question, 'Where does the bend go?' the answer is that we have three choices. We either release it and straighten up for a tall majestic finish, we allow the bend to become a twisting under, or we maintain a constant hip angle well into and beyond impact, allowing the head and shoulders to move on through. The choice you make, of course, will be whichever one you relate to best.

THE PLANE OF BACKSWING AND THROUGHSWING

The plane of backswing and throughswing for any golfer should match. The overall plane should preferably follow the angle of the club shaft at address, certainly for all but perhaps the very tallest of players.

The angle we see in the club shaft at address we should again see in the left arm at the top of the backswing. The club should then return through impact in much the same position as it was at address and then move into a follow-through where the club shaft once again takes up this angle. If we look at the simplest of golf swings, this is what we see. The movement seems easy because everything is coordinated. The club starts on one angle, returns to that angle through impact and then continues through on very much the same angle.

The angle of the clubshaft in the followthrough should match its angle at address. Most club golfers never get through to this position

The angle of the club shaft in the follow-through can tell us a lot about the swing. Conversely, working at the angle of the club shaft in the follow-through can steer the club into a better 'position' through impact. From your address position, which we will also assume to be the impact position, take the club directly through to your follow-through without any backswing. A reflection in a mirror or windows should tell you whether the club is on plane. If the club moves into the correct kind of position, the odds are that the swing is fairly good. In achieving this, the arms should be relatively close together in the finish, not forced into any contorted position but with the elbows at roughly the same width as at address.

If, as is the more unusual of the two, the club has adopted too vertical a position with the club shaft very much down the back, the clubface has possibly been held open through impact with the arms moving into too upright a plane. The arms will have worked very much away from the body, with a real up-and-over feeling to the follow-through. The question with this movement is whether it has matched the backswing. If the arms have lifted high in the backswing – as in that of Nicklaus or Watson – only then should they come through and up-and-over in the follow-through into a plane that matches.

More of a problem is for the player who produces a plane of follow-through which is flatter than the address position and flatter than the backswing. Tom Watson's backswing is great, providing it goes with Tom Watson's follow-through! But if it went with Bernhard Langer's or Lee Trevino's follow-through it would be none too clever. The important point is symmetry.

Try to retain a simple concept of the swing with the club moving in a continuous movement, and realise the plane of swing you are looking for.

An overly flat plane to the follow-through can be produced in two ways. The first is for the right arm to work very much over the left, closing the clubface through and beyond impact, left elbow folding in and right one working over it. In this position the back of the right hand would be relatively flat in the follow-through, with more likelihood of drawing or hooking the ball away to the left. The wrong but more common way of getting a flat follow-through is for the player to allow the arms to spread beyond impact. Instead of the left arm folding away correctly, it tends to come into impact with the elbow bone facing the target, the elbow buckles outwards rather than folding inwards and the flat follow-through sees the left elbow flying out behind the player. This sort of elbow spread tends to encourage a follow-through where the club comes flat around the head or neck, and often goes with holding the clubface open. For an advanced golfer this tends to produce erratic direction.

Generations of golfers tend to follow the best players of their age. Nick Faldo, with what is almost a handicap of being so tall, has to work continually at flattening his swing rather than allowing his shoulders to drop under and the swing to become steep. If anything he appears to err on the side of being flat in the finish rather than more upright. Players tend to copy this. But what they don't appreciate is that when professionals make this movement the elbows are close together, the left one working very close to the right rather than the arms spreading. The correct movement through should see the left arm fold out of the way, forearms staying close onto each other. The arms then move into the correct plane of throughswing with the left elbow very much in front. The easy but

If the followthrough appears flatter than the backswing, with the elbows together, left arm well forward and under, the likelihood is drawspin to the left

If the flat followthrough is the result of the elbows spreading the clubface is inevitably being held open – for pros like Joakim Haeggman intentionally, for amateurs often producing unwanted slice

wrong way of finishing is to allow the arms to spread, with the left elbow trailing out behind.

So learn to see the overall plane of your swing and ensure that the finish really does match your address and impact position. Swing the club on a continuous curve and a constant plane.

THE RECOIL – YOUR SAFETY VALVE

Never assume that the follow-through is unimportant, and don't simply assume that a good follow-through is the result of a good shot. The thought should be that *aiming* for a good follow-through and producing it increases the likelihood of a good shot. The advantage of working with the follow-through is that we can take the learning out onto the golf course. Your brain is still moving forward and at the end of each swing you get feedback from the movement produced.

One essential part of the follow-through is balance. Top-class players need to produce a follow-through where the legs and shoulders are totally balanced and stationary until the ball touches down. It can easily be held for several seconds. Indeed, a marvellous exercise is to hit a ball and hold the full finish until the ball is on the ground. Although it seems a long time, the ball is probably in the air for a maximum of only 8 to 10 seconds. But those 8 to 10 seconds give tremendous feedback and comprise a real safety valve. As an exercise, play a few holes and hold the follow-through at the end of every swing for a count of '1, 2, 3, 4'. Counting out loud ensures that you breathe and relax. It also confirms whether your follow-through really is balanced and as comfortable as you imagine. The right knee should have slotted round towards the left leg, and the balance on the left foot should be easy. But in reality, the scratch golfer is unlikely to hold the follow-through for 4 seconds on the course. In many ways, if he did, performance would probably improve.

What is important is that the movement away from the follow-through is precise. What should *not* happen is for the hips to want to spring back towards their address position. The hips and legs should feel that they lock on through to a balanced position very easily. Correctly, from the follow-through the next movement is for the arms to drop back down to the side, elbows to the waist, arms still bent. The player should then watch the ball in a perfectly balanced position with the club up in front of him. This recoil is far more important than most people imagine. It is the safety valve in the swing. The player swings through into the follow-through, and from there the legs and hips stay locked, the shoulders stay still and the arms drop back down to the side. Watch any professional golfer watching his own good shot and you will see this position. The legs should then stay perfectly balanced until the ball touches down. Consistently producing this position *encourages* good shots.

The recoil is important; it ensures balance long after the ball has gone. It encourages a repetitive position and it also means we get feedback from the follow-through. If the follow-through is good, the recoil should feel easy. The elbows simply drop back down to the side and the club shaft will be sitting directly up in front of you on target. If the follow-through has been wrong, particularly with the elbows spreading and the left elbow flying, the recoil feels awkward and the left elbow will want to recoil out to the side instead of directly down towards the waist.

The tidier and more repetitive this movement the better. The aspiring tournament golfer should aim at being good in practice for 8 seconds beyond the ball and in ordinary play a good 6. Stand and watch the ball and make sure this position is balanced and consistent. This allows for the swing to deteriorate when the player is tired, nervous or under pressure. Very few players swing as well on the golf course as on the practice ground, and very few swing as well under pressure as they do in ordinary play. If the follow-through is at all untidy, errors soon emerge in a pressure situation. By working at a follow-through which is balanced and a recoil which is repetitive the player has every chance of making that same swing under pressure. If his balance is there for 8 seconds

From the followthrough the arms should drop to the side, still bent, legs perfectly balanced and shoulders still. If the finish is good the recoil should feel easy – and easily held until the ball lands. The player's view sees the club vertically in front of him, clubface square. It is this position that promotes consistency under pressure

A more complicated finish –
in this case Anders Forsbrand
playing for a cut. The recoil
is proof of the open faced
action, left elbow wandering
away to the side

on the practice ground and 6 in general play, even at his worst he should still retain balance for a good 2 or 3 seconds. But if the follow-through doesn't have this precision, the moment the wind blows fiercely or the tournament is all-important the swing can lack that winning edge.

PUTTING THE BRAKES ON – TWO STEPS TO POWER

The follow-through is like the brakes on your car. If the braking system is poor, you won't generate speed. But for the low-handicap golfer the follow-through can sometimes simply become untidy. Particularly for young golfers, the swing can become loose and the follow-through erratic.

The swing requires two surges of power. The first is to deliver speed into impact and the second is to put the brakes on firmly and sharply to produce a balanced finish. It shouldn't be just a gradual slowing down but a definite feeling of a punchy, controlled finish where the balance is perfect. This is particularly important for the smaller player who has less stopping space than the tall golfer. It isn't a question of decelerating, of course, but one of accelerating fast through the ball and then finding the strength to lock into a perfect, stationary, controlled finish.

STATIONARY SHOULDERS IN THE FINISH

The top-class player should stamp out any shoulder action at the end of the swing that indicates where the ball has gone. Many players, professionals included, finish the swing and then allow the right shoulder to come up because they see the ball drift away to the right. The assumption is that this is simply an after-effect of seeing the ball going off-line and is only a harmless movement. The danger is that the player tends to associate this right-shoulder movement with the ball drifting away to the right. Sooner or later he gets to a point where he sees out of bounds or a lake on the right side of the course and the right shoulder begins to be active *before* the ball is struck. Sure enough, the ball slides away to the right and the shoulder comes up. But the roles of cause and effect have probably switched.

To my mind this is the difference between Tom Kite and Tom Watson. Watson swings the club through into a perfectly stationary position every time. The shoulders never move and one never gets an impression of where the ball has gone. The swing is perfectly consistent and there seems no room in his swing for a bad shoulder movement into or after impact. Tom Kite, by contrast, went year after year looking like winning major championships, before eventually winning the 1992 US Open. He was constantly in contention, only to carve the ball away into trouble on the right, with the right shoulder coming up to signal disaster. Was the right shoulder a 'result'? More likely it was the cause.

Work at a finish that is perfectly stationary, and where the shoulders are virtually level. Make the swing look good with a shoulder position which never indicates your displeasure at the direction of any shot.

Remember that what you see as the innocent after-effect of a bad shot can easily become its cause.

SYMMETRY OF ARM ACTION – SHORTENING THE LEFT ARM

In every swing we make, the right arm folds away in the backswing and equally the left arm folds away in the throughswing. The extension in the swing beyond impact is the length of the right arm from right shoulder to the club shaft. Once the club gets to waist height in the throughswing the left arm must occupy a relatively small space. Bear in mind that the right hand is beyond the left. If the left arm stays too straight, the right one cannot keep up with it without the right shoulder being forced either round or underneath. The feeling must always be of the left arm shortening away.

In effect, the movement of the right arm in the backswing is repeated with the left in the throughswing. The problem for many players is in letting the left arm get out of the way correctly while still remaining in control. The left arm is in control in the backswing and delivery, then all of a sudden through impact has to fold away at speed to allow the right one to move through. Very often with medium- and higher-handicap players the left arm folds the wrong way. Instead of bending and folding inwards, it arrives at impact in a rigid position and then buckles. Club golfers often see pictures of themselves beyond impact and are concerned to see their left arm bowing outwards. They seem to believe that the left arm at this point should be straight, and see the fault as the left arm bending. The more they attempt to get the left arm straight the worse it gets.

There are two things that can happen if the left arm stays too rigid on impact. The first and more common is that it simply buckles and bends outwards. This sees the player working through into the follow-through with the arms spread. The player whose left elbow tends to fold or buckle outwards beyond impact almost always holds the back of the left hand and the face of the club uppermost beyond impact, with the clubface held open as it strikes the ball. Instead of working from toe-up to toe-up the player tends to work from a toe-up delivery position into a face-up position beyond the ball. The face is held open and the elbows spread. This, as we will see later, is just the position we want in bunker shots and some of the short game where the back of the left hand is held very much upwards, the elbows should spread and the clubface in turn is held open. But in the long game it is just what we want to avoid. The left elbow should fold in, forearms closing onto each other with the arms staying close.

The danger for the good golfer is that if the left arm stays too rigid the wrists simply flap on the end of rather straight arms, rolling the clubface from open to closed over a short space through impact. Direction tends to be erratic, often with a hook under pressure. Unfortunately the player often thinks hooking is lack of control with the left arm and tries to keep it even more rigid, and in turn the hook worsens.

The left arm must shorten beyond impact in every shot we play. Folding and breaking inwards encourages a square or closing clubface; folding or breaking outwards encourages an open face.

The more active the hips through impact in relation to the arms and club the more likely the player is to fade or slice

TIMING – THE RELATION OF BODY AND CLUBHEAD

The whole golf swing is a question of coordinating and timing the turning of the body and the swinging of the arms. Let's look at a relatively loose, free swing rather than a tightly coiled one. The body turns to the right in the backswing and the arms do their lifting. From here the arms swing down and up the other side while the body turns through. The movement is a turn and a lift, a turn and a lift, but the timing is crucial.

Some top-class players are more likely to fade the ball and others to draw it. The grip may be the same and the swing may be fairly similar, but the key to which way the player is likely to spin the ball is often a question of how the body and clubhead move in relation to each other. The player who is quick with the turn through of the hips in relation to the arms and clubhead is more likely to fade the ball. This action taken to extremes produces a slice. The player who is slower in the legs and body in relation to the arms and clubhead will tend to draw the ball, his bad shot usually being a hook.

The player who fades the ball will usually lead on through impact with the hips and have a feeling of hip clearance ahead of the hands and clubhead. The clubface is held square or fractionally open at impact – just a degree or two – while this hip slide pulls the clubface across the ball through impact, imparting the tiniest of cutspin. It is not a question of swinging out-to-in but simply, at the moment of impact, the rapid pulling away of the hips just sliding the clubface fractionally across the ball. If the hip movement gets too rapid the pull across the ball with the clubface is exaggerated and the shot may turn into an unwanted slice.

The difficulty is that the timing of body and clubhead is often exactly the opposite of what we feel. A player who tends to fade the ball probably dislikes a hole with water or out of bounds to the right of the green. Instinctively, however, he may aggravate the tendency to go there by spinning the hips away even more quickly, as though trying to keep the ball away from danger. This simply adds to the cut-across feeling through impact and may exaggerate the cut. Rather than spinning the hips through more quickly, the feeling should be of holding the legs back a touch and allowing the arms and clubhead to get there in time or even slightly earlier.

By contrast, the player who tends to draw or hook the ball will usually be slow with the legs and quick with the hands, the arms and clubhead moving fast and freely past the legs. Sandy Lyle and Tom Lehman are prime examples of this. If anything the clubface closes as it goes through impact and the shot may become a draw or in some cases a hook. If the legs block and work insufficiently, the hands and arms are forced to scissor over each other and the clubface closes, possibly producing a quite pronounced hook.

For the advanced golfer who hooks, the problem is often one of insufficient hip, leg and body clearance when fighting a fear of hooking. The player who draws or hooks the ball usually dislikes holes with out of bounds running down the left of the fairway. As he stands on the tee he shies away from the left side of the course. At this point he is even more likely to block with the hips and legs; the arms and hands take over and the clubface closes. Instead, the feeling needs to be of standing up and spinning the hips into the shot, so that hips lead and clubhead follows. In this way the clubface is more likely to be a touch open and the ball can safely move slightly

Those who draw or hook the ball are often slow with the legs and hips in relation to the arms, allowing the clubface to close if the body lags behind

left-to-right. The moment it leaves the clubface the player will know that the ball is either moving straight or with a touch of fade. But for many it is instinctively difficult to speed up the hips and almost turn the body towards the trouble zone, in the desire to move the ball away from it.

The feeling of timing will vary from one player to another. The player who fades or cuts the ball often has to have the feeling of holding back the legs, hips and shoulders and speeding up the arms, hands and clubhead. The player who draws or hooks the ball will often have to feel a very pronounced spinning through of the hips to keep everything moving on song. Timing for some can be crucial. The difference at impact may be minuscule, but just letting hips get slightly ahead of clubhead or lag slightly behind the clubhead can result in slight errors of direction and unwanted spin. The timing of the turn of the body and the movement of the arms can be paramount.

SQUARE TO SQUARE OR SHUT TO OPEN

Professionals invariably teach beginners to move into a takeaway position at hip-height where the toe of the club points directly upwards, back of the hand facing outwards. From here the player can cock the wrists upwards as the backswing continues. This same position is usually repeated in the downswing and the player is then encouraged to find the mirror position beyond impact, left arm beginning to fold away, toe of the club again pointing upwards and the back of the right hand facing forwards. In other words, the clubface moves from 'square to square'. In fact the body bends over slightly from the hips at address and the correct position for the advanced golfer is for the toe of the club to be slightly forward of this toe-up position. The true toe-up position for a top-class golfer is perhaps marginally open.

The essence of swinging the club from a square position in the delivery to a square position in the throughswing is to allow the arms to turn, forearms rolling onto each other if anything, rather than to put emphasis on the wrists. The universal use of the larger, American-sized ball has almost eliminated the feeling of hand action for most top-class golfers, the ball getting airborne and taking up backspin far more easily.

But undoubtedly many top-class golfers play all their golf with the clubface moving from slightly shut to slightly open. In the takeaway the clubface stays looking a touch more downwards than our toe-up position, and as the clubface works into and beyond impact it stays looking fractionally upwards. For many this gives a better feeling with iron shots, the clubface seeming to move into a slightly straighter path back and through impact. The feeling of a slightly open face beyond impact ensures a touch more backspin on landing.

The important point is that the clubface must move symmetrically through impact. It either moves square to square or it moves from slightly shut to slightly open. Many tournament professionals like to hold the club-

The clubface should move symmetrically in backswing the throughswing. In theory the club moves from square to square – works with both irons and words and is generally considered the most orthodox method

face slightly open on their medium and short irons and will therefore instinctively hold the clubface fractionally underneath in the takeaway to allow this to happen. It is the thought of the delivery and impact that dictates the takeaway rather than vice versa. The player probably has no feeling of doing this, but in thinking of the way the clubface moves through impact will automatically compensate in the takeaway.

The low-handicap golfer who swings from shut to open on every shot will usually be a strong medium and short iron player who often faces difficulties with the longer clubs. For first class golf the feeling of being able to move the clubface in both ways is essential. The key is to ensure that the positions just before and just beyond impact mirror each other and go hand in hand.

Many pros hit their short irons with a shut to open action – the clubface being held under in the takeaway and upward beyond impact. It is a movement more suspect with the longer clubs and generally unsuitable with driving

Sometimes we see a player who gets into a shut position at the top of the backswing purely and simply because the grip is wrong. With a perfectly square clubface we ideally see the face of the club following the line of the left arm at the top of the backswing. The player whose clubface is shut adopts a position where the clubface looks more up to the sky than it should. If it is a grip problem the simple way of steering the player towards the correct grip is to allow him to take up his position at the top of the backswing, then to ask him to loosen his hands to adjust the position of the club until it looks correct, and to have him regrip.

THE FOREARMS AND THE CLUBFACE BEYOND IMPACT

More errors for advanced golfers are caused by the clubface being slightly misaligned through impact than by anything else. The player doesn't have problems of clubhead speed or contact and will usually start the ball relatively straight. But errors of the clubface usually produce the unwanted sidespin of the crooked shot.

Ideally for a perfect, straight shot the clubface must be perfectly square to the target and line of swing through impact. Several degrees out through impact with an iron and you can still hit the green; one or two degrees out with the driver can spell disaster. But feeling the precise clubface 'position' through impact is far from easy; everything is moving at such tremendous speed. What we can feel, however, is the clubface 'position' beyond impact. Working at that position can often correct what happens at the ball.

If we translate a clubface which is a tiny bit open or a tiny bit closed at impact into a position at hip-height beyond the

A slicer **does** this and holds the clubface open

He needs to do this with a square clubface

ball the difference is far more pronounced and much easier to feel. Let's assume the club approaches the ball in a square position halfway down the downswing, toe of the club upwards. The corresponding square position in the throughswing is again toe-up at hip-height. The feeling of an open clubface beyond impact is one where the face of the club looks upwards at hip-height, and the feeling of a closed clubface is one where the face of the club looks downwards.

For the top-class golfer there is always an element of fine tuning and making the clubface do just what you want. One day or one week it may feel as though the clubface is being held a touch open, and another day or week it may feel as though it wants to close. It is a question of feeling the clubface and making tiny adjustments as necessary.

Very often the player who leaves the clubface open needs to feel the clubface move into a face-downward position beyond impact. The feeling here is of the forearms rolling onto each other, left arm folding away and the forearms closing. If the forearms work onto each other the face of the club feels to be face-downwards at hip-height, and as this is continued on through to the follow-through the arms must once again stay close to each other. The feeling may almost be of the right arm climbing over the left and the left elbow being pulled tightly in against the right arm. The clubface feels to be face-down beyond impact and will still

He needs to **feel** he does this and closes the face

be slightly face-down by the finish. If the arms work onto each other the clubface tends to close. The feeling may be very slight or quite pronounced.

The problem for many club golfers is that the left arm gets in the way. I often teach players who have been good at some racquet sport. I give them a squash or tennis racquet and ask them to show me the movement of cut-spin or topspin. The feeling of cutspin, of course, is of the right wrist staying back on itself and the right hand never rolling over after striking the ball. The feeling of topspin, by contrast, is of the right arm turning over. I then suggest to the player that he takes hold of the racquet in both hands, rather like a golf club, left hand above right, and reproduces the same feeling. The feeling of cut is very easy, but at first the feeling of topspin is difficult. Suddenly the left arm blocks and feels as though it won't get out of the way. The feeling for the player who fades the ball is just like our racquet player suddenly putting both hands on the club. The left arm feels in the way, and while the cut action and open face are still quite possible, the feeling of topspin or our equivalent of drawspin becomes difficult.

If we want to draw or hook the ball, the feeling is very definitely of the forearms rolling onto each other, the end of the swing seeing the left elbow pulled in and downwards as though under the right arm. Players who produce a flattish plane of swing often believe they swing like Bernhard Langer or Corey Pavin. But instead of seeing the elbows pushed onto each other, they wrongly allow them to spread. The closer the forearms stay to each other through and beyond impact, the more likely the player is to draw the ball or indeed the less likely to cut the ball. The more the elbows spread beyond impact, the more likely a fade or cut. The feeling for the top-class player wanting to fade the ball is very often that of the left

Correcting a slice. The player who fades or slices tends to hold the clubface up beyond impact. He often needs to **feel** that the clubface closes into a face down position beyond impact, like Ian Woosnam's, and stays face down as long as possible in the followthrough

hand leading to resist it turning over. Conversely, the feeling in trying to produce draw and maximum run for a driver or 3-wood from the tee is of the arms staying tight together through and beyond impact, but with the left rotating away.

Conversely, the player who is troubled by hooking or drawing the ball more than he would like may need to feel the clubface being held slightly upwards beyond impact, possibly now with a feeling of the forearms spreading a touch beyond the ball. By aiming at this feeling beyond impact the clubface is controlled into the ball.

When we want to hold the clubface open, the feeling is of the back of the left hand staying uppermost beyond impact. With the back of the left hand upwards, the left elbow tends to point slightly towards the target and the forearms begin to work apart. It is precisely this movement we want to see in a bunker shot; the left elbow will almost slide away behind the player, short-

The player prone to hooking tends to close the clubface beyond impact. His feeling needs to be of holding the clubface square (or face up) beyond impact and to work at height in the finish. The followthrough follows the toe of the club. The club must have moved through a toe up position beyond impact to achieve height in the followthrough

ening and spreading. The right wrist stays hinged back on itself and the clubface works upwards. The feeling of holding the clubface open through impact is of the arms spreading; the feeling of draw is of the forearms working together.

A player trying to discourage a hook or draw and attempting to fade the ball should move into impact allowing the hips to turn fairly rapidly to the left while the arms continue straight ahead. They don't, but that is how it *feels*. In other words, we get separation between the hips spinning through and the arms swinging on up. The feeling is simply of the arms swinging the club out towards the target and then folding up and away. Providing there is sufficient lift with the arms in the throughswing it is virtually impossible to hook from a sound grip. Too much separation tends to lead to a slice. The player who draws or hooks the ball will usually have a feeling of togetherness beyond impact. The hips don't rotate particularly quickly and if anything the arms tend to scissor round towards the body and stay fairly close. The follow-through will if anything produce a slightly flattish arm plane, elbows

together; the whole feeling through impact is of the body and arms working very much together. Imagine an extension from the club shaft pointing to your belly button throughout the impact zone. As the body turns through, so the club moves through. There is no particular feeling of independence of the arms and certainly not of the hands and wrists.

By contrast, the player who fades the ball will have this very definite feeling of separation, of the body going round and the arms going up. Again it is a question of understanding the feeling of both movements and using one or other as necessary to produce the fine tuning need to produce good golf.

This part of the swing is far easier to feel than impact itself. First of all, impact is still an acceleration zone while the throughswing sees the club decelerate. We also get feedback from the end of the swing on the movements through impact. If the arms have worked onto each other, elbows fairly close, the odds are that the clubface has more chance of closing through impact. If the arms have spread and the back of the left hand seems to have worked upwards, then the clubface may well have been held a touch open.

The two shots also require different relationships of the body and arms. A player who fades the ball will usually get separation between his hip action and arm action beyond impact. The player who draws the ball is far more likely to work the two together.

No golfer ever gets to the position where the swing feels as if it will stay entirely constant. But here we begin to understand how to make the necessary adjustments. The player who is more worried about cutting the ball needs to work everything together beyond impact. The player who tends to draw or hook the ball needs that feeling of separation, as though the hips are spinning out of the way and the arms are moving upwards. For clubface control, see the aim of correct movement beyond impact as producing the strike you want.

6

THE SKILL OF SHOT-MAKING

DIRECTION – WHERE DOES IT START? HOW DOES IT SPIN?

The main problems for the advanced golfer are normally directional ones. The club player's difficulties of poor contact or poor flight are usually minimal for the good golfer.

The first key to good shot-making is to be able to start the ball straight on target

Essential in correcting the direction of shots is to separate the two aspects of direction. Firstly, where does the ball start? Secondly, how does it bend or spin? If the good player starts the ball bang on line every time, he is unlikely to have a disaster with the shorter clubs. But with the longer ones even a degree or two out with the clubface through impact can lead to a costly error.

It is important to isolate the two factors. Sometimes a player sees his shots drifting away to the right and is not really clear in his own mind whether the ball is starting there or spinning there, or a combination of both. Similarly, the player trying to correct a slight fade may strengthen his grip and begin to hit shots to the left. He assumes the grip change is over-done. In reality he is probably simply starting the ball left expecting it to fade back to the right but now hitting it straight there with a grip that is good.

For players with a spin problem the clubface should always be corrected first. Get rid of unwanted spin and then tackle the direction of the swing. But for the good player, being able to start the ball on target every time is crucial. This is largely a question of adopting a suitable ball position – too far forward and you can easily start it left; move onto it and you can just as easily start it right. A good ball position must then be combined with accurate aiming with feet and shoulders, and a perfect awareness of the target while playing the shot.

DOES THE OUT-TO-IN SWING REALLY CAUSE A SLICE?

The theory books all tell us that an 'out-to-in' swing causes a slice. I have my doubts that this really is the case. Certainly an out-to-in swing *aggravates* a slice, but on the whole I believe more golfers swing out-to-in *because* they slice.

A professional golfer swinging out-to-in is far more likely to pull the ball straight left. If loosening up with the whole right side of the body he may in addition close the clubface and produce a snap hook. The out-to-in swing does, of course, cause a slice only if the clubface is open to this path. In practice most club golfers start life with a swing that is too steep and possibly right side dominant. They tend to be stiff in the wrists, and hold the clubface open through impact and beyond, by failing to let the wrists or arms turn over to square up the clubface. By hip-height in the through-swing the clubface is usually still uppermost, the left elbow uppermost and if anything the left arm breaking outwards rather than folding inwards. Correctly the club should be in a toe-up position by hip-height in the throughswing, or even with the feeling of being slightly face down. The player sees the ball drifting away to the right; as any sane person would do, he tries to steer it to the left. But instead of trying to keep it left with the clubface he starts aiming the swing left with his shoulders and possibly ultimately his feet. Swing and clubface become even more across each other, and a slice develops.

We then, of course, associate an out-to-in swing with the slice, but in reality it is usually the clubface error that causes the problems.

Exactly the same can apply to the scratch golfer. The clubface starts to be held open for some reason – perhaps a weak left-hand grip or the fear of hooking. The ball drifts away to the right and the player subconsciously starts counteracting this by allowing the clubhead to move slightly across the ball through impact. The out-to-in swing is there only because the clubface is being held open. In tackling the problem we must always start first with the clubface and then correct the path of the swing.

CORRECTING A SLICE OR FADE

The player who leaves the clubface a touch open will inevitably start swinging slightly out-to-in. For the good player this may simply mean that the club attacks the ball rather straight down the line instead of from the inside and then pulls in across the back of the ball. He may not be out-to-in as such but is certainly not meeting the ball sufficiently from the inside.

The clubface should always be tackled first. It is far less effective to start by tackling the direction of the swing. If we work at the direction of the swing it may improve on the practice ground but certainly won't work on the course. If the player tends to fade the ball to the right, with a driver or 3-wood for example, it may certainly ease the problem in practice to encourage him to attack the ball more from the inside. As soon as he gets on the golf course with trees or out of bounds down the right side of the hole, however, nothing in the world is going to induce him to hit the ball with a feeling of an in-to-out swing as though starting the ball into trouble. The only way an in-to-out action is going to feel possible is if he can actually associate it with draw. That takes time.

Far more effective is to correct the clubface through impact so that the player begins to pull the ball. He needs to be made more aware, or even possibly afraid, of the left side of the course. If he fades the ball the odds are that he stands fractionally left. He may also play the ball too far forwards. If the fade can be turned into a pull he usually begins to correct his stance instinctively. He starts to query his own aiming and soon moves himself on target. If he worries about the left side of the course rather than the right, he will feel comfortable in playing the ball further back in the stance and hence will start to contact the ball from the inside.

Occasionally even a single-figure handicap player can be hampered by a pronounced cut or slice. I always make the first correction if necessary to the grip, totally ignore any misalignment of the shoulders or an out-to-in swing, and get the player able to bend the ball to the left. Often this is a completely alien feeling. It is a question of working the clubface through into a position where it can close through and beyond impact so that the player can feel both ends of the spectrum of spin. If he can feel a slice and can now feel a hook he can begin to work at something in the middle. If he can experience only the cutspin then it becomes very difficult to find a straight shot. If the slicer can be made into a puller or a pull hooker, worrying about the left side of the course, then the fault can easily be corrected. I usually suggest that he goes away and loses plenty of golf balls on the left side of the course with an altered grip or altered hand action, until it is the left side of the course he fears. Only after this happens should he begin to square up his stance and alter the direction of the swing. The swing path then becomes relatively simple to correct. The player now wants to start the ball out to the right, wants to attack it from the inside, wants to stand square and wants to play the ball further back in the stance.

The player may have suffered 6 weeks of agony and lost a few golf balls on the left side of the course, but by tackling the clubface first the swing-path problems are much easier to correct.

THE GAME OF SPIN AND CURVES

Golf is very much a game of spin. Certainly in other sports the ball spins, but the problem in golf is rather different. In other games the ball tends to travel in the direction you hit it. Then, as you get better, you learn to put spin *on* the ball. The problem with golf is that the dimple construction of the ball is there to encourage the ball to take up spin. It needs spin, of course, to get airborne. But just as the dimples are there to encourage back-spin, so they very easily produce sidespin. The initial problem is to learn to take that sidespin off the ball to produce a straight flight. Then the good player can learn to put spin back on again.

A slice with a golf club is like a cut shot with a racquet. The racquet face is held open and the ball caught in front of you with a firm-wristed, up and down, action – producing a shot which cuts and stops. With a golf ball on the ground most people's instinct is to swing up and down and produce cut more easily than draw

Most new golfers, having played some other sport reasonably well, have one or other spin already at their disposal. Most tennis players can play a forehand cut shot very easily, while others find topspin far easier. The tennis player who cuts the ball usually becomes a slicer with a golf club. The player who is more of a topspin expert can usually associate with the feeling of a draw or hook. Similarly, in kicking a football the feeling can be one of putting cutspin or hookspin onto the ball.

Frequently even low-handicap golfers don't associate the feeling of a draw or fade with spin with another ball game. As soon as they can relate the two it becomes far easier to correct a spin problem or to learn to put on both forms of spin.

Let's look at how spin with a tennis racquet relates to our golf shots. First of all, a forehand cut shot. The whole idea is a shot that lands and pulls up fairly lifelessly, leaving the opponent short of time and speed to get to it. It is a dead, weak shot. Just the same applies to a cut shot with a golf ball; it takes off distance and speed. Playing the shot with a racquet, the ball is collected from well ahead of you, the right wrist is held back on itself, the racquet head remains upwards and never turns over. Backspin and cutspin are imparted to the ball. The action is an up-and-down one. If you added the left hand to your racquet, holding it double handed, but left above right like a golf club, you could still play the same shot. The action with a golf club is much the same. It is predominantly an up-and-down action, firm in the right wrist, clubface held open and backspin and sidespin imparted. You can make a similar movement with the golf ball on the ground as with the tennis ball in mid-air. The racquet head or golf club is swung up and down and across the ball.

Now let's look at the topspin forehand and see how that relates to the golf shot. The whole idea in imparting topspin is that the ball bounces on forwards with maximum speed. The racquet now meets the ball possibly

A draw or hook with a golf club is like topspin with racquet. The ball is caught from further behind you, racquet head moving up and over to create topspin. The difference with a golf ball is that it sits on the ground. The direction of the attack feels the same, but with a downward not upward attack

further behind you, is swung more round behind your body and moves on up and through with the racquet face downwards and turning downwards as it makes contact with the ball. By the end of the swing the right arm has moved on through, racquet always in a downward position. The movement is shallower and more rounded, racquet face turning over as the ball is struck. Now try this with a double handed racquet action, again left hand above right. The feeling now may be that the left hand and arm get in the way of making the same movement.

When looking at a draw or hookspin with a golf ball we are looking at the same type of movement. The swing, in just the same way, is a more rounded one behind the body, and the club-face attacks the ball with a curved path and must be allowed to turn on over as the movement goes through. Just as our racquet face looked down as we followed through, so the clubface must seem to look down as it moves through to waist height beyond the ball. Once more the left arm must get out of the way to allow the right one to turn through.

The underlying difficulty in feeling this with a golf ball is that in golf the ball sits on the ground. With a tennis racquet we are trying to make topspin on the ball by actually coming up and over the ball and catching it with an upward movement. In golf we are trying to make the same curved path but cannot get beneath the ball for an upward strike. (Possibly we could with a driver from a peg but let's ignore that for the moment.) We are trying to hit the ball on the same curve but we still have to meet the ball with a downward delivery. Correctly with a golf ball we are not, of course, putting on topspin. The ball must still take up backspin to get airborne. But we are trying to make the same kind of *directional* attack to move the clubface out across the ball. The reason why most golfers feel more at home with a cutspin type action than a topspin action is simply that the ball is sitting on the ground. Cutspin with a racquet is an up-and-down action. Topspin with a racquet is a down and up-and-over action.

To feel the movement of topspin and drawspin, hold your club out in front of you as though attacking a ball at knee height. From here you should

To feel drawspin with a golf club hold the club out at knee height and feel the topspin action of racquet shots. From here learn to feel the same roundness of the action in making contact with the ball

be able to imagine a topspin movement and the required curve. Now make some practice swings that make contact and brush the ground with the same feeling.

If you are a golfer who can experience only one of these spins, experiment with the feelings learnt from racquet sports. If you are a squash player, a hook is like a low smother into the bottom left-hand corner of the court; a cut is like holding it away into the upper right side of the court. With the first we see speed and with the second possibly softness and control. Relate the two. Take your racquet onto the driving range to get the feel if necessary, but allow yourself to learn from past experiences with other games.

To feel draw on the ball the arms need to stay together through and beyond impact, left elbow well in and forward. The clubface stays face down beyond impact

DRAWING THE BALL

It is sometimes suggested that drawing a ball is wrong for a top-class or low-handicap player because it can easily become a hook. Certainly the top-class golfer doesn't want to draw the ball with most of his iron shots into the green. The ball would lack sufficient backspin. But for many golfers drawspin is more natural than fade and can help to produce maximum length.

Another view of the same action – this time the right hand now off the club, but showing clearly the arms closing onto each other, clubface still slightly face down at this point. An action for the slicer to copy en route to correction

There are two ways of drawing a ball. The first one – and to my mind the wrong one for the good golfer – is simply to allow the clubface to close slightly through impact. The feeling is that the clubface turns over at the moment of impact. The action may be slightly one of hands and wrists, feeling a wrist roll through impact. This is an action frequently seen with junior golfers who are relatively loose in the limbs. This kind of draw certainly can easily become a hook. The player who draws the ball in this way, particularly with a 3-wood or driver off the tee, needs to be very firm in the wrists, with just a suspicion of the arms turning over through impact so that the clubface, although closing, is perfectly in control. It should certainly feel one of arm action rather than hand and wrist action. Players who play in this fashion often tend to stand off to the right of the target, start the ball out along their feet and then bend it back towards the target.

Corey Pavin playing a draw – right arm climbing over the left through and beyond impact, clubface still facing downwards well into the followthrough

The more correct way of drawing a ball for a top class player requires no emphasis on hands and wrists. The feeling is one of the clubface being wiped slightly across the ball from in-to-out and therefore producing sidespin. Just as the top-class player can produce cutspin by moving into impact and then sliding the clubface left across the ball to produce cut, so he should be able to produce draw by easing the clubface out across the

The safe way of drawing the ball is to address it slightly from the toe, to keep the clubface square to the target through impact and simply to feel that the clubface moves in-to-out across the back of the ball to impart sidespin. From here the feeling in the throughswing can be of the clubhead moving out and up beyond impact into a high finish, guarding against the draw turning into unwanted hook. Relate it to spin with a table tennis bat or racquet

ball in the opposite direction. To feel this the clubface is held on target at address and the stance is square. The feeling is of taking the club away perhaps a little more on the inside than usual, with the clubface still looking on target for the first 12 inches or so of the takeaway. In other words, the clubface is held slightly hooded. The ball should preferably be addressed slightly towards the toe of the club. Now in the attack, the feeling is of the clubface moving out across the ball from toe towards heel, so that beyond impact the clubface moves out a touch, still square to the target and producing the sidespin. The clubface doesn't turn over but simply imparts spin by moving in-to-out across the ball. It is, of course, only fractional. The attack needs to be a shallow one. Beyond impact the arms should stay fairly tight together and move on through quite naturally.

The player who draws the ball in this way will start the ball slightly out to the right of the line of his stance and turn it back in towards the target. The ball will bend only 2 or 3 feet in the air and the result is, in effect, a straight draw. The feeling of spin is there. The player knows immediately the ball leaves the clubface that it won't drift away to the right; the curve, however, is really apparent only to him and anyone standing directly behind. The beauty of this shot is that on landing it allows for maximum roll. The clubface is firmly on target through impact and wrist action is kept to a minimum.

Although the clubface will be held slightly differently in the takeaway to feel draw, the thoughts should simply be forward ones, feeling the forward action of clubface moving across the ball. The takeaway usually adjusts itself slightly to accommodate this feeling.

The top-class golfer who draws the ball usually spins the ball in this manner. He simply wipes the clubface from in-to-out across the ball, addressing it a touch in the toe and starting it away slightly to the right of the line of the feet. Those who teach draw and who are not natural drawers themselves sadly often associate draw only with wrist roll and for that reason see it as a dangerous shot to be avoided.

Played well, the draw can be just as accurate as the fade for all but the shortest of iron shots, and it has the advantage of penetration into a headwind or wind from one's back.

The player who fades the ball and is encouraged to swing from in-to-out will find it effective only if his thoughts are of imparting sidespin to the ball. If you can feel the clubface move across the ball in this way and associate it with a shot that spins slightly left, only then should you take any thoughts of trying to attack the ball from the inside out on the course with you.

DO IN-TO-OUT SWINGERS HOOK OR HOOKERS SWING IN-TO-OUT?

I asked the question earlier whether out-to-in swingers slice or whether those who find themselves with a slice begin to swing out-to-in. Precisely the same question arises with a hook.

The theory goes that if you swing from in-to-out you will hook the ball. This, of course, is a fallacy. If you swing from in-to-out the usual result is a whacking great push away to the right. But the only player who produces a hook from swinging in-to-out is the player who wipes the ball with the clubface, moving from in-to-out across the ball as described earlier. In this case the player would have to take the club back very much on the inside, keeping the clubface on target, i.e. hooded, and then have a real feeling of sidespin.

In fact, what usually happens is that a player develops a hook, often as a child, and usually as a result of a poor grip where the right hand is underneath. As he comes into impact the clubface naturally closes and every shot bends, possibly quite severely, from right to left. The player will then do one of two things, or sometimes a combination. Firstly, he begins to aim away to the right, as any right-thinking person would, in an attempt to keep out of trouble on the left. Usually both feet and shoulders are aimed to the right. The player then simply starts the ball out to the right and hooks it back in. We hear people saying that he is attacking the ball from in-to-out. Certainly the attack is in-to-out in relation to the proposed ball-target line but is not in-to-out in relation to his stance. It may indeed be out-to-in in relation to his stance and he simply adjusts the stance to start the ball where he wants.

What may begin to happen is that the player starts looping the club on the inside and does actually develop an in-to-out swing. In other words, he still probably aims off to the right but then tries to start the ball even further right in his frustration at seeing it go left. He probably drops the right shoulder in, produces a rather unusual inside loop, and still sets the ball off to the right. The more he goes on like this the worse it tends to become, and the ball can end up swinging the whole width of the fairway. The ball takes up a lot of bounce as it lands, not suddenly turning and bouncing straight up the fairway, but of course continuing to bounce to the left.

The usual remedy is one of changing the grip until the clubface can be squared up. The player then finds himself blocking the ball away to the right and will hopefully start aiming away to the left.

The player who corrects a hook, usually with a grip change, often unfortunately continues to think of himself as a hooker for many years to come. He may rarely if ever hook again, but the tendency to aim off to the right remains, and he may well miss far more fairways by pushing the ball to the right than he ever did by hooking.

The important correction for the player who hooks is to change the grip if necessary and to feel that the clubface can be held upwards a touch beyond impact rather than turning over. Then, having learnt to control the clubface, he has to learn to start the ball on target. One of the best exercises is for the player to hit balls on a driving range (where the mat will encourage him to stand squarely) with a light garden cane or closed umbrella 15 feet or so ahead of him and a couple of inches to the right of the target line. He then needs to practise religiously starting the ball left of the cane, working at the feeling of the clubface, to cure his instinct of starting the ball out to the right and waiting for the hook that will hopefully no longer happen.

Colin Montgomerie playing a soft landing iron shot, with a touch of cut, clubface held up through impact, back of the left hand resisting

SOFT LANDING IRON SHOTS

The low-handicap player who hits strong fairway shots is often troubled by getting insufficient stop on the ball. Firstly, this is a question of being realistic about when you can get backspin, and secondly, it is learning the technique to achieve it.

Remember that even the best professionals don't achieve backspin downwind on a fast running course. Nor do they achieve backspin when hitting up to a flat, elevated green where the ball isn't landing vertically. Tournament conditions seen on television are sometimes very different from those at ordinary clubs. American-style greens are often banked quite acutely from front up to back, are constructed of sand and well watered and are indeed receptive. But having said that, the professional golfer is undoubtedly able to produce more backspin than many a single-figure handicap player.

Nick Price holding the face open and cutting one in

In order to achieve backspin the feeling is very close to that of producing a touch of cutspin. Remember that with a medium or lofted iron the ball cannot actually be seen to move from left to right, but the touch of cut is there. The contact needs to be crisp, striking the ball and nipping out a tiny divot. The clubhead doesn't simply bury itself in the ground but moves through with a very definite in-and-out action. The clubface has to be held fractionally upwards beyond impact, with a fairly firm back to the left hand. If anything, as the clubface moves into the ball it pulls fractionally away to the inside and therefore imparts a touch of sidespin. The left elbow may almost drag away slightly to the left, with the arms not exactly spreading but certainly not rotating onto each other.

The back of the left hand pulls in and out sharply through impact until the feeling of backspin develops but with no noticeable drift in direction away to the right.

LOFT KILLS SIDESPIN

A common pattern of shots for longer-handicap players is to pull the ball left of target with the medium and short irons and to slice the ball quite violently right of target with the driver. The player often imagines that the swing is completely different with one from the other. In habitually leaving the clubface open with the driver he starts to swing from out-to-in in a vain effort to keep the ball left. The slice worsens. With a lofted iron the out-to-in swing still happens. The open clubface produces far less sidespin and the ball flies straight left.

It is as though a ball will take up only so much spin. With a lofted iron there is so much backspin that there can be no room for any sidespin to

These two pictures of Peter Baker and Ben Crenshaw show the different action beyond impact of cutting a ball in or moving the face through squarely for minimum spin. Notice the position of the right hand and wrist – still cocked back in holding the clubface open, far flatter for a square face

take effect. With the straight-faced clubs there is relatively little backspin and therefore potentially more sidespin. Another way of thinking of it is to imagine yourself spinning a dinner plate. Stand the plate up in front of you and put your fingers at its centre. Spinning it is easy. With your fingers way below its middle, spin becomes difficult to achieve.

The lesson for the low-handicap golfer, worried by any hook or slice problems, is to use a club with adequate loft where accuracy is all-important. A narrow hole of 360 yards may require a driver and a 9-iron or it may require a 5-wood and a 7-iron. For many players, the accuracy level with a 5-wood is dramatically different from that of the driver. Obviously, most golfers are more secure the nearer they get to the green. But when length is not necessary a more lofted wood can pay dividends. The temptation in facing a par four 50 yards longer than you can drive is to try to thrash the ball to get it there. It can't be done. Using a 4- or 5-wood loses perhaps only 20 yards and adds enormously to accuracy.

Many club golfers also look for drivers with far too little loft. Some players are tempted to use drivers with 7 degrees of loft. Remember that Bobby Jones had 8 degrees on his putter! There is a dramatic difference in accuracy between a driver of 7 degrees, 9 degrees and 10 or 12 degrees. As soon as loft is reduced, potential sidespin is increased.

Remember, conversely, that when you want to produce bend on a shot, perhaps holding the ball into a cross-wind, the straighter faced the club the more easily sidespin can be achieved. A punch shot with a 5- or 6-iron really can be bent into the wind; the loft of a 9-iron or pitching wedge kills the potential sidespin.

So remember that if sidespin ever becomes a problem, the easiest way of killing it is to use more loft.

DRAWING AND FADING THE TEE SHOT

Ideally we all like to hit the ball straight with minimum of bend. There is nothing more satisfying than drilling the ball straight down the middle of the fairway and seeing it hold its line perfectly.

When the fairway is very narrow, however, a ball with a touch of fade or draw can be more accurate. If you drive the ball slap down the middle of the fairway, potentially you have only half of it to work with. If a little inaccuracy creeps in, the margins are very small. If on the other hand you can accurately fade the ball, with a suspicion of bend left to right, the feeling can be of starting the ball down the left of the fairway and having the whole fairway to work with if the bend takes effect. Similarly, the player who draws the ball can start the shot down the right side of the fairway knowing perfectly well that the ball won't move right but will only, if anything, drift left. The great South African Bobby Locke worked on the principle that by hooking the ball – as he did with every shot – he gave himself twice as much room to work with as the player who aimed down the centre.

If you are not comfortable fading or drawing the ball, it is better attempted with a 3-wood than a driver. Using our lesson that loft kills sidespin, it means that the bend with the 3-wood is unlikely to be overdone. A fade is more likely to turn into a slice or a draw into a hook with a driver.

In order to draw the ball with the tee shot we can tackle it in one of two ways. The first is to feel the forearms staying close to each other, if anything closing over on to each other through impact; the clubface can be felt to be slightly face down as it moves through the waist-height zone beyond impact. The feeling will be that the face continues to look down very slightly, moving on through to a finish where once again a face down position can be seen and felt. The left elbow feels close into the right and if anything tucked in and under the right, but with the arms long and extended.

The second way of feeling the draw is to address the ball a touch towards the toe, to feel that the clubface is held on target in the takeaway and to wipe the clubface in-to-out across the back of the ball to feel a touch of spin. The first method perhaps gives the feeling of starting the ball straight and allowing it to turn to the left. This may give more feeling of starting the ball slightly right of the line of the stance (and target) and bringing it back in. Obviously it is a question of adjusting the stance if necessary to start the ball where you want.

To encourage draw with a driver it sometimes helps to tee the ball slightly higher than normal, encouraging the feeling of staying behind the ball and if anything being able to hit slightly on the upswing. This then enables the player to have a feeling a little bit more like the topspin racquet shot. The ball can in effect be caught slightly on the upswing with the idea of a more rounded, shallow attack. There can then be a feeling if necessary of leaving a little more weight on the toes of the right foot at the end of the swing with the impression of producing overspin – in fact simply minimising backspin – adding a touch of draw and run.

Most tournament professionals like to tackle a hole with trouble down the left by being able to stand towards the trouble and work the ball away from it. Again, there is a feeling that you have more space to work with. The ball can, if you like, drift the whole width of the fairway, giving more leeway than simply aiming down the middle. This is particularly important for anyone prone to drawing or hooking the ball under pressure. The feeling should be of choosing a definite spot down the left side of the fairway, aiming the clubface at it or a degree or so right of it, feet and shoulders aiming where you want to start the ball. For most top-class golfers the feeling is simply one of holding the clubface a touch open through impact, which means slowing down any turnover of the forearms. In effect the back of the left hand may feel to block a touch.

For the tournament golfer to add a touch of fade to a drive the simplest way is to tee the ball a touch lower, to move the right thumb more down the front of the grip and simply to speed up the legs and hips a shade in relation to the clubface. The difference shows in the finish

For the player nervous of hooking, it can help to position the right thumb more down the front of the club, with a little downward pressure – a minor adjustment, but one that helps immobilise the wrists and if anything encourages a slightly open face through impact. The lower you tee the ball, the more likely you are to move onto the shot and again hold the clubface slightly open, squashing the ball away to the right and protecting the left. If teed up high, the temptation is to hang back and if anything close the face. So knock the tee in a touch further. The third essential is to ensure that the hips are lively enough through impact, clearing the body well so that there is a separating relationship between the body spinning through and the clubface and arms. In other words, the hips spin through while the arms feel as though they go straight ahead. Some players need to feel just the tiniest bit of holding the clubface open to achieve this. Others need to work at the grip, hips and how they tee the ball. To others, standing a touch taller can give the feeling of standing above the ball on a sidehill lie and thus promote the likelihood of a fade. It really depends on how easy or difficult you find this shape of spin. But remember, again, that if there is a danger of the fade turning into a slice, the easier loft of the 3-wood can give far more control than a very demanding driver.

WHY FADE THE DRIVER?

Many low-handicap golfers can play every club in the bag reasonably well apart from the driver. Suddenly, perfectly straight shots turn into ones that bend quite dramatically to the right. Part of it, of course, is the simple element of reduced loft. But frequently it is a question of changing a player's concept of the drive and dispelling a few myths and theories.

We are usually told that the ball should be played towards our left instep with a driver. The bottom of the swing should still fall opposite the player's nose and the ball is then ideally collected on the upswing. The problem for many is that by pushing the ball out towards the left foot the direction of the swing is lost. The bottom of the swing doesn't still fall correctly opposite the player's nose, with the ball several inches beyond it. What happens is that the bottom of the swing gets too close to the ball, the player often wanting to tee the ball down instead of high, and the path of the swing starts meeting the ball on a slightly out-to-in path. In other words, it has simply been dragged away to the left by the time impact is reached. Occasionally this will cause the player to have a snap hook, but more commonly he simply holds the clubface open and produces a slice. The further forward in the stance the ball is played the less able he is to swing the club in a rounded path. The attack becomes steep instead of shallow.

When faced with a low-handicap player who fades or slices his drives I ask what he would expect with a 3- or 4-wood from a sidehill lie with the ball above his feet. He would, of course, expect it to bend away to the left. As soon as you put the ball, let's say, at knee-height the feeling is of draw

Why fade the driver? The low handicap golfer who has an unwanted fade with the driver should tee the ball high and think of a sidehill lie, weight slightly back on the heels, ball not too far forward and with a rounded swing. Holding the clubhead fractionally off the ground (as many pros do) encourages a shallow takeaway and attack. From this type of lie (and action) one would draw rather than fade

and not fade. The answer is in the ball position. If faced with a sidehill lie there is no instinct to play the ball further forward in the stance. If anything the tendency is to play the ball in the middle of the stance, be forced to swing round and round by the angle of the slope and with it produce the draw.

I therefore suggest as a remedial exercise that the ball is teed up really high, positioned only slightly ahead of centre, and that the player sits well back on his heels at address and says to himself, 'sidehill lie'. Immediately the ball flies off with a lower, more penetrating path and the feeling of draw may be experienced. When you look at many top-class professional golfers you will often see more of this action. Many don't tee the ball particularly well forward in the stance but in fact play it several inches back in the feet. Often I assume they are using a 3-wood and probably not a driver, but even with a driver, the ball is frequently nothing like as far forward as theory would suggest.

The player who perseveres with this problem by using the 3-wood and constantly reminding himself of a sidehill lie soon finds that he can hit the ball with the flight he wants and that the fade disappears.

The difficulty in using the driver is that it often seems to have too little loft. The feeling may be subconscious, but as soon as the player puts it to the ball the feeling of a rounded swing tends to be lost. In approaching impact there may be an instinct to add loft to the clubface. He begins holding the clubface upwards as it strikes the ball and it continues to look upwards beyond impact. Instead of moving into a position which would be toe-up, waist-height beyond impact, the clubface still looks upwards. The player is probably subconsciously unhappy with the loft of the club and, in trying to make loft, holds it open. This is just what we would do with a sand iron but with the sand iron, the sidespin is killed. Hold the face up on a driver and the sidespin is all too obvious.

Many golfers hit high slices with a driver through having a club with too little loft. Through impact they instinctively try to hold it open through not trusting the loft. With a lofted driver they would feel more able to keep the face square or closing for draw and a **lower** flight

The tendency is for the player to see the ball going high and to the right and assume that he needs to use a club of less loft and to tee the ball lower. In reality if he had a club with *more* loft he would stop struggling to make loft on the face through impact. A lofted club would encourage the player to feel the arms turn over a touch through impact, as though almost trying to keep the ball down. Suddenly the feeling of draw becomes feasible.

The tall golfer, of course, is often at a disadvantage when learning to drive well. The taller you are, the more there is a feeling of standing above the ball. Nick Faldo is a foot taller than Ian Woosnam. Put Ian standing on a slope a foot above the ball and he would unquestionably feel prone to slicing. Put Nick standing a foot below the ball and he would feel himself likely to draw or hook. So, particularly for the tall golfer, the feeling with the driver often needs to be of sitting well back on the heels, avoiding squatting because of the difficulties this causes in finishing the swing correctly, but still working on a flatter and shallower plane of swing and a more rounded attack.

So, if a fade from the tee is your problem, use a club with sufficient loft – don't try to make loft as you meet up with the ball – tee it up high, pull it back in your stance and keep reminding yourself of a sidehill lie.

THE DRIVER – START DOWN TO HIT UP

The takeaway with the tee shot should be shallow and inside. We need to work at a rounded shape of swing in order to produce a rounded attack.

In trying to relax at address it is easy to hold the club and arms almost too loosely, sitting the club on the ground without really having control of it. You need to make sure that the club is hanging from the arms and shoulders, touching the ground if you like but not resting on the ground without your support. With the driver, such looseness and relaxation can often lead to the club being picked up very slightly in the takeaway. The weight of the club is gathered and the shoulders can lift and tense up a touch. The shallow path tends to be lost.

For this reason you will often see professional golfers holding the driver fractionally off the ground. This ensures that the player has perfect control – he isn't just resting his club lifelessly. It also means that he can take it away with a smooth, slow, shallow takeaway, all of which encourages the feeling of roundness.

A common problem with driving is of playing the ball well forward in the stance and then bringing the bottom of the swing to the ball rather than staying behind the ball and hitting it on the upswing. Holding the driver fractionally off the ground encourages a downward takeaway and hence an upward attack. It gives the feeling of being able to stay behind the ball and to tee the ball up high enough with confidence.

STARTING THE BALL STRAIGHT

Being able to start the ball straight, particularly with a driver, is vital. If you can practise from a driving range mat, setting yourself up identically each time, an excellent exercise is to place two small cans 12 or 15 feet ahead of you, about 9 inches apart, and working at trying to drill the ball out on target.

To someone watching even the best of golfers from behind, a directional error will often show up within the first 18 inches to 3 feet. The ball can easily be 2 or 3 inches out within that first yard.

Perhaps the most important key to producing good direction is to ensure that there is a clear picture of the target firmly in the left side of your head throughout. At the moment of impact you are not hitting the ball to the target but to the *picture* of the target in your head. Many club golfers appear to have no picture at all in their heads. Professional golfers undoubtedly do have a picture of the target area, but for some it is presumably far clearer and more definite than for others. We see some players with a near-perfect swing who lack instinctive direction, others who very rarely stray off line.

Good direction is a combination of good alignment, possibly choosing a spot to aim over (and choosing this accurately), and then knowing instinctively where your target is.

FAIRWAY WOODS – LIKE STRIKING A MATCH

Many low handicap men find fairway woods more difficult than long irons. For women just the opposite is true. Generally this is as a result of setting up incorrectly, usually by pushing the hands too far to the left at address. The club then sits on its front edge, the back of the clubhead up, and the strike becomes a downward, ball-divot contact. This is just the technique for squeezing the ball away from a divot or slight depression with a 4- or 5-wood, but not from a good lie.

For good fairway wood shots the clubhead should always sit flat on the ground, club shaft pointing to your belly button rather than your left shoulder. Except for shots from the fluffiest of lies, there should always be one or two practice swings to feel the contact of the sole of the club bouncing on the ground. The feeling is one of slapping the sole plate down and up – a short, light, very definite contact, like striking a match. Players who have a marked lateral movement through impact often find this contact alien. The back of the clubhead comes up; the head now has a cutting edge instead of a bouncing bottom.

The fairway wood requires a sweeping type of swing, with less 'suddenness' through impact than an iron, an action or timing that top women golfers often find easier.

GRIP CHANGES THROUGH THE SET

I know of many top-class golfers who don't use quite the same grip for their iron shots or fairway woods as with the driver. With the iron shots one does if anything move onto the ball, making the ball-divot contact. The more you move onto any shot, particularly if the lie is bare or hanging, the more likely you are to squeeze the ball away to the right. The clubface is probably left a degree or two open as you move fractionally onto the ball for a good contact. By contrast with the driver, there is no sensation of having to nip the ball out or move onto the ball. Just the reverse. If anything you hang behind the ball, possibly meaning that there is more likelihood of meeting the ball with a slightly closing face.

For this reason you will often see players with a slightly more neutral or weaker grip with their driver than with their irons. In other words, the hands are more to the side of the club with the driver, in a slightly weaker position, the Vs between thumb and index finger pointing fractionally nearer the chin than with the irons.

With a poor lie the tendency to leave the clubface open will sometimes be counteracted by the player simply closing the clubface fractionally at address. Others will instinctively strengthen the grip a touch to allow more lateral movement through impact while still starting the ball on line.

The grip change may be very small and so instinctive for the tournament professional that he is hardly aware of the adjustment. The difference is in the contact you feel and rehearse before playing the shot. The driver and fairway wood, with a sweeping attack, have a much steadier, continuous delivery – a feeling of hitting past yourself. A neutral grip, erring on the weak side, will still square up the clubface. A point to watch is that in weakening the grip the shoulder line is still correctly right shoulder below left and not becoming too horizontal. With the ball-divot contact of an iron (or a fairway wood from a poor lie) the more one envisages moving onto the ball the stronger the left hand may need to be to bring the clubface through squarely. There may, indeed, be a feeling of working the clubface from fractionally shut to open – a sensation that is less productive with the sweeping contact of a drive than with the ball-divot contact of an iron.

HITTING A LOW DRIVE

The easiest way of hitting a low drive is not necessarily to tee the ball down. For some players, it works; for others, the very fact of teeing the ball lower encourages a steeper, more downward blow and increased backspin.

Certainly the ball should not be teed particularly high, but it should still be well off the ground. The feeling then is one of hitting the ball cleanly from the top of the tee, concentrating on leaving the peg in the ground. In this way it is as though only the top 90 per cent of the ball is caught; backspin is kept to a reasonable minimum and the ball should produce a penetrating flight into the wind.

For some players the feeling needs to be of minimising any wrist action. Players who have a predominantly hands and wrists method often hit the ball high and find a low shot demanding. A good concept is to imagine that the club shaft points straight up towards your belly button, and that the whole swing away from the ball and through impact is played with the end of the club always pointing towards you. The takeaway and delivery should feel as though body and club work very much together. Practising a takeaway to waist height and a movement through the ball, both with this feeling, before playing the shot will often do the trick. The backswing feels as though it will be short and stiff wristed, but in reality the swing will freewheel itself to much the same backswing position as normal. The hands are likely to remain more passive through impact. This adds width to the impact zone, and helps to reduce the action of hands and wrists whipping the ball up into the air.

ELEVATED GREENS AND BASIN GREENS

It is always more difficult to stop the ball with backspin on a green perched above you. The ball won't have completed its full trajectory and meets the green travelling more horizontally than usual. The danger of an elevated green is that on one day you might hit, for example, a 7-iron which finishes right at the back of the green. The next day you therefore decide on the 8-iron only to see the ball fall short into the bunker guarding the green. In reality the 7-iron shot probably only landed a yard or two onto the plateau but inevitably ran on through. The ball probably pitched the correct distance but the contour of the ground produced added run. The key is to get the maximum possible height to the shot, adding a little cutspin if you can.

Remember that an elevated green may also drain more freely than other greens on the course. The ground is often firmer, holding less moisture, and the run is inevitable. If playing to an elevated green from an uphill lie, the slope tends to add loft and backspin for you. If playing from a tee or other flat lie, watch for the danger of underclubbing and expect to be at the back of the green. The challenge is making the score from there.

With a green in a basin we get the opposite effect. Not only does the green gather moisture, being receptive anyway, but the ball is also landing more vertically and has every chance of stopping.

The difficulty with a basin green is that we are generally approaching the shot coming down a hill. If you pitch the ball short of the green it tends to bounce and kick through. If you can make yourself bold enough to pitch the ball right onto the green, it will often hold. The danger is that we see the ball land short and jump through and so become more cautious. If by contrast you can persuade yourself to fly the ball right into the heart of the green, you will often find these the easiest shots of all to hold and some of the most satisfying to hit.

SLOPING LIES

The golden rule with sloping lies is that the ball always follows the slope of the ground. An uphill shot hits the ball up, a downhill lie keeps it down. If standing below the ball the ball would run down the slope to the left. It will turn to the left in the air and then kick left. If standing above the ball it would roll away to the right. It will turn to the right in the air and spin that way on landing.

The difficulty of the sidehill lies depends on your natural shape of shot. Those who hook hate to stand below the ball; those who slice generally dislike standing above the ball. The slopes bring out the worst in these players. The key is to allow enough to the side, not only for the ball to turn in the air, but also to take up spin. When standing above the ball, the crucial factor is balance. The slope brings you in closer to the ball, makes the swing more upright and tends to throw weight forward onto the

Standing above the ball brings you in closer, steepens the plane of the swing and produces push and fade. Good balance is crucial, remembering that the ball not only bends to the right in the air but spins that way on landing. Most golfers underestimate the drift right

balls of the feet, so balance must be maintained. The same pattern will follow for both short and long shots. With the ball above the feet, the distance from the ball increases, the plane flattens and the tendency is to drag or draw the ball to the left. Particular attention needs to be paid to short shots on these lies where it is easy to forget that the ball may turn substantially to the left.

With a downhill shot the problem is that the ground gets in the way. Loft tends to be reduced and the ball moves away to the right. The key here

RIGHT: To control an iron shot from an uphill lie the stance needs to be narrow – often uncomfortably so – standing vertically. In this way the player can climb on up the slope through impact with little difference to the flight of the ball. If instead the shoulders follow the slope, hanging back through impact, the ball flies high and left with little control

is to adopt an address position with the right shoulder as high as possible, shoulders following the slope. The stance needs to be really wide. The feeling is of swinging up and down the slope, the follow-through travelling down the slope beyond impact. The left knee will bend or sink, never straightening up. The right shoulder must be kept high throughout to avoid striking the ground behind the ball. The loft is reduced, the amount depending on the degree of slope, and care needs to be taken to aim well left to allow for the ball to drift right.

The uphill shot can be one of the most difficult for pros; the upslope adds loft but it also tends to send the ball away to the left. The usual advice is to follow the same pattern as for the downhill lie, shoulders following the slope. But in reality this is not how most pros tackle an upslope. More common is to stand vertically, shortening the left leg as necessary, and simply trying to swing as normally as possible, back and into and up the slope. The key with an upslope tackled in this way is that the stance must on occasions feel unpleasantly narrow. The feet need to be close enough together to allow the feeling of climbing up onto the left leg through impact and into the finish. If the stance is too wide there is a tendency to hang back on the right foot and see the ball dragged away to the left. If the feeling is of climbing up the slope and producing a firm balance on the left leg, the ball will fly very much as normal. If you hang back, it goes left; if you overdo the movement through, the ball may push a shade right.

AIMING LEFT

Many players have difficulty in aiming across the set line of a tee or fairway. The usual problem is from a tee on the right side of the hole where the player has difficulty in aiming towards the middle or left of the fairway. The same problem also arises when trying to aim left to allow for the wind on your back.

The key point is to ensure that you really do choose the target. It is often easy to be half-hearted and lack commitment in your choice. You choose a tree to aim towards, but in reality you don't want the ball to go there. You probably choose something further left than you imagine and set the clubface and feet at odds with each other.

The first point is to be precise about where you *want* to hit the ball and to mean to hit it there. You mustn't choose a target further left than you want while in reality hoping the ball finishes somewhere different. Players with this problem will understand what I mean.

First of all, choose the target. Make sure that the clubface really does aim there and keep the feet parallel to that. It is very easy to aim the clubface in one direction and then to aim the feet and shoulders left of it, setting up a cut rather than a shot that flies straight where you want. If anything the feeling for most players has to be of keeping the clubface a touch left of the line of their stance. Having chosen the target, really do whole-heartedly *mean* to hit the ball there.

Indecision can often arise when trying to aim left of a bunker or tree. You aim 20 or 30 yards left of it but in reality mean to be only 5 or 10 yards left of it. The choice of target must be consistent.

In trying to aim left down the fairway it is always worth remembering that the further you tee up on the right side of the teeing ground, the more you can aim across the fairway and away from trouble. You can get a completely different view of the hole by teeing up on the right, in the middle or on the left of a tee.

The practice swing with a drive can also help. Instead of simply standing a few inches away from the ball for a practice swing, try moving behind and to the right of the ball, in other words more towards the ball and the tee box, and make the practice swing there. Moving this extra couple of yards can often make a more definite feeling of aiming the whole practice swing left and can sometimes help with alignment and the choice of target.

7 THE ART OF PUTTING

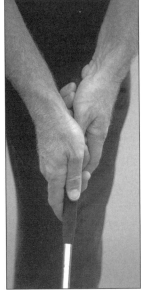

The standard reverse overlap grip for putting – used by over 90 per cent of pros – and popular for over sixty years. Peter Baker and Nick Faldo

THE REVERSE OVERLAP GRIP – THE WEAK LEFT HAND

The standard putting grip is, of course, the reverse overlap. It is one that has been in use for at least sixty years. Probably 95 per cent of professional golfers use this grip, and although there are variations to it, there are also very definite guidelines.

Firstly, put the left hand on the grip in what amounts to a weak position. In other words, the left hand should not be predominantly on top of the club. The shaft and grip should come up through the fold at the top of the left hand rather than running through the palm or fingers of the hand. This means that the shaft of the club and the forearm should be reasonably lined up together and the wrists will sit high. Having put the left hand on in this way, the left thumb should be virtually down the front of the club.

The key to getting a good reverse overlap grip is the positioning of the right hand. As the right hand is put on the club it can go on in one of two ways. The first way, and to my mind the correct way, is to ensure that the heel of the right hand is brought against the middle finger of the left. The left index finger is, of course, going to hang out eventually so let's get rid of it at this point. The heel of the hand now rests against the left middle finger or two fingers and the right hand can fold over. The left index finger is then draped around the outside in a comfortable position, most commonly over the third finger of the right hand. The key point is that the right hand is *outside* the fingers of the left hand rather than below them. This means that the hands can work in unison. It also means that both hands are predominantly to the side of the club.

The second way of positioning the right hand on the club is to put the right hand beneath the fingers of the left. This, generally speaking, is not as good. The hands if anything will work against each other, allowing the left wrist to kink as the club goes through.

If you look down at your own grip in the correct position, the hands will appear fairly open. The left thumb *does not* fit in the palm or pocket of the right hand. The grip is an open one with a definite gap to be seen in the fold of the right hand. Now the hands can work well together without the feeling of the right taking over. The pads of both thumbs are of course on the front of the club, and whether or not one puts the right index finger down the club is a matter of personal preference. Gene Sarazen christened this 'the after forty finger grip'. But for golfers, old and young, it can add both feel and control.

ABOVE LEFT: The author's rather smaller hands show the relationship of the right and left hand. Correctly the heel of the right hand should rest lightly against the second singer (or second and third fingers) of the left hand. The fingers are slightly inside the palm of the right hand with he left thumb visible down the front of the club

ABOVE RIGHT: Wrong. This is a reverse overlap grip but with the left hand too far over and the left thumb in the pocket of the right hand rather than down the front of the club

HIGH WRISTS AND LOW WRISTS

Generally speaking a high wrist position at address is more accurate than a low wrist one. The rules of golf say that a putter has to have at least 10 degrees between the shaft and the vertical; a putter that sits completely upright is not permitted. If you get a club with an upright lie and hold the wrists high at address, the putter can sit in an upright position. The easiest way for most players to keep the putter moving in a straight path, for a short putt in particular, is to hold the wrists high and the club shaft up at this angle, hands directly beneath the shoulders.

If the club sits with its toe off the ground, the shaft of the club is lowered. The more of an angle the club sits at, the more likely it is to be swung in a round and round path.

A player like Ballesteros who holds his hands low at address is in fact setting up to swing the putter in a curved path. To keep the putter swinging in a straight path he has to make tremendous shoulder movements to keep the clubhead travelling on a down-and-up path

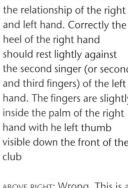

Jack Nicklaus with a very 'open' grip, allowing the wrists to arch and stay high. **Both** thumbs are very visible

Tom Watson with a rather stronger left hand grip, perhaps the source of some of his recent putting woes!

through impact rather than turning away to the left. Seve is obviously a genius at what he does and gets away with it. But for most people, holding their hands low at address means that there are inevitably certain putts where the clubhead does turn to the left and the ball in turn is dragged away.

One reason for so many golfers playing in a position with low wrists is that they use putters which are probably too long for comfort. Logically it doesn't make sense for a player of 5 foot 8 to be using the same length putter as a player of 6 foot 4. If his putter is too long, and his hands are at

Tom Watson and Peter Baker showing the classic high wristed position of good putters, elbows in and wrists arched up, putter head sitting flat on the ground

the top of the shaft, he will either allow the left wrist to show too much kink at address or he will push his hands down at address and with it force the toe up. In this position the eyes are very unlikely to be directly over the ball. Some players unquestionably find it easier to see the line of a short putt without their eyes over the ball, but in the main it tends to produce a tendency to drag the ball away to the left.

In order to feel a high wrist position, hold the club out in front of you, preferably with a reverse overlap grip and with your elbows slightly into the sides. Check that the left hand is in a weak enough position, both hands seeming to be under the grip of the club and with the left thumb very definitely not fitting snugly into the palm of the right hand. From here, have the feeling of keeping the forearms still and tip the clubhead by arching the wrists. From there bend over in this position to feel the wrists sit high.

If the left hand is allowed to get too much on top of the club, so that the club shaft runs through the palm of the hand and under the heel pad rather than up through the crease of the hand, this high wrist position becomes difficult. The more beneath the shaft the hands are held the easier this high wrist position becomes. Look at Jack Nicklaus for an example of a player whose hands and wrists sit very high at address for putting, and for the openness of the grip.

Seve Ballesteros and Isao Aoki in toe up positions at address, wrists low. These positions require plenty of upward shoulder movement through and beyond impact to keep the putter moving on a straight path. The tendency from a low wrist position is to turn the putter left through impact, an address position often caused by using too long a putter

Tom Watson, putting at his best, adopts a very high position. When the left hand gets slightly stronger, his wrists drop. I also think the shape of the putting grip makes a difference. The curved-over grip, like the Ping grip, encourages high wrists. A totally flat-fronted grip with no shape perhaps does not give as definite a feeling. Remember that from this position it is easier to get your eyes directly over the ball and the line of the putt. For most people this encourages a good, straight stroke for sound short putting.

EYE LINE AND AIMING

There are four key factors to good short putting, the first of which is aiming. It is, of course, crucial. Many golfers consistently tend to aim to one side or the other. Often a putter with a line on it makes alignment easier. The Ping or Zebra putters with a long line from front to back are perhaps some of the easiest to line up squarely.

Seve with a very smooth putting stroke, the angle of the left wrist staying constant through impact and the left shoulder working up to keep the putter square – a pendulum. Think 'tick, tock'.

It is certainly worth checking from time to time that you do aim straight. Sit the putter to the ball, steady it with your left hand and walk round behind the putter to check the direction. But what if you don't naturally aim straight? The more common aiming problem seems to be of aiming right rather than left. The player who aims off to the right, perhaps as much as an inch outside the right lip on a 3-foot putt, usually finds the short right-to-left putt particularly difficult. The natural tendency is usually to aim to the right and drag the putt left and this simply doesn't work on a side slope.

The first check point is the eye and head position. The eyes should in theory be directly over the ball and the head horizontal. This in theory will give the best view of the putt. For a longer putt the head can swivel rather than turning. The difficulty is that players who are right-eye dominant often find this view awkward. The very short putt of up to 30 inches may not cause problems; beyond this the view of the right eye is restricted and the player is forced to use the left eye or start turning the head to bring the right eye into action. Sometimes the player will find it easier to aim if the eyes are not directly over the ball. By moving the head back, i.e. so that the eyes are now over a spot inside the ball-to-hole line, the player gets a clearer view of the putt as though slightly in front of him rather than

beneath him. Aiming may suddenly seem easier. The problem now, however, is that there is a tendency to hold the hands and wrists low at address and more danger of the putter describing a slightly curved path and pulling away to the left through and beyond impact. But certainly a change of head and eye position can help.

A good way of checking your alignment is to set up three spots on the green – a ball, a coin or marker 12 to 18 inches away and directly on line with the third object, a tee peg. From behind the ball, set the three in a perfect line. Now adopt your address position. If the three still stay in line then you are unlikely to have an aiming problem. Frequently, however, the marker will seem to be displaced to the left, perhaps an inch or so, meaning that your tendency is to aim an inch or so to the right of this. You simply don't see a straight line. If the marker seems displaced to the right then the odds are you tend to aim left. If this is your problem – and it is a fairly common one – there are three courses of action open to you. The first is a trip to the optician. Find one who understands golf, explain the problem and see if he can assist; some can. The second course of action is to practise repeatedly until you are convinced that the three points are in line. The third remedy is to experiment with your head and eye position to see if the problem can be solved.

FINDING THE SWEETSPOT

The second key to good short putting is to hit the ball bang off the sweetspot. Assuming good aiming, this is probably the next most important. It is relatively easy to monitor and yet it is often ignored.

The advantage of a Ping type of putter or a centre-shafted putter is that it gives a relatively large sweetspot. An ordinary blade putter will often have a fairly small, sensitive sweetspot. Many players don't strike the ball consistently on the clubface. The Ping style of putter or centre-shafted putter is unquestionably more forgiving. To check the sweetspot, hold up your club lightly from thumb and index finger and, tapping with your fingernail or tee peg, work from the toe of the club through to the heel. Initially you feel twist in the putter head. You then come back to a point where the putter seems to swing straight backwards and forwards, before coming to a spot near the heel where the twist is felt again. The larger this area of no twist, the larger the sweetspot.

Having checked the sweetspot, monitor your accuracy of strike. A good exercise is to mark the sweetspot with a tiny sticky label and to practise striking the ball from it. Another is to put a couple of small rubber bands round the putter head, giving yourself half an inch hitting area between them. Again you can soon tell if you are striking the ball accurately from between the bands.

Striking the ball slightly towards the heel of the club is one of the most common reasons for short putts spinning away to the left. Particularly with a blade putter, the strike can be very sensitive. The nearer the ball is struck to the toe, the more likely the ball is to spin away to the right. The more in the heel, the greater the chance of the ball spinning left.

THE SQUARE CLUBFACE

The third factor is to strike the ball with a perfectly square clubface. Most players place far more emphasis on the direction of the stroke itself than the contact. And yet, in reality, the stroke has far less bearing than the squareness of the clubface to the hole at impact. Obviously a good stroke is aimed at returning the clubface squarely to the ball. But it is hard to monitor and feedback from missed putts doesn't usually point to the true error. If the stroke is bang on target but the clubface fractionally open or closed this shows far more error than a square clubface with the strike a touch off target. The clubface is the dominant feature of the two.

There are many great putters who don't use a square clubface and a straight stroke. As with the golf swing if you aim for a square face it can err towards being closed or open with errors both ways. If you consistently err on the side of an open face – as many good putters undoubtedly do – it gives just one source of error. It is the closing face which is the more dangerous and common on bad short putts. So, although not something one would teach, the feeling of putting with the face a touch open and of slightly cutting the putts is not without merit.

My favourite 'square face' exercises is to practise putting with a cotton reel or short piece of metal pipe, filled with lead tape to roughly the weight of a golf ball. It will only roll straight if met with a truly square face!

Another way of monitoring the squareness of the face is to practise with a ball, painted with a narrow stripe. Practise striking the ball until you can roll it correctly, over and over, along its stripe. Any tendency to leave the putter face slightly open or closed soon shows up with the ball rolling slightly awkwardly.

Nick Faldo with a straight back and through stroke for a 6 foot putt, eyes directly over the ball, stance square, head horizontal

SHORT PUTTING – LEFT SHOULDER UP, BALL IN THE CUP!

The fourth factor is the direction of the stroke. Although important the direction of the strike has far less bearing than the square clubface and a strike with the sweetspot. While working at the stroke it is these two which should be kept in mind.

Some players like to think of the short putting stroke as a straight line. Others see the clubhead as going back slightly on the inside and then straight through. Certainly you don't want the club moving back on the outside. Tucking the right elbow in a touch at address can encourage a straight or inside path.

Tournament greens are unquestionably much faster and truer than they were twenty years ago. Players putting on slow greens or greens with heavy grain, such as in South Africa or Asia, often adopt a putting stroke where the hands are pushed forwards and the stroke is a slightly downward one. This pops the ball away firmly. The feeling with this is of keeping the clubhead low to the ground beyond impact.

It is now more generally accepted that a better stroke is to hit the ball at the very bottom of the swing or slightly on the upswing for a truer roll. Trying to keep the club moving downwards through impact will often tend to bring it round to the left. The feeling of an upward stroke through impact often helps to keep the putter on line.

The movement through must be combined with a firm back to the left hand. Possibly the worst technical fault with a putter is to allow the left wrist to break. The upward movement is ideally produced with the shoulders. They should be perfectly square at address, encouraging this by keeping the right elbow in. In the throughswing the left shoulder should work upwards, the whole unit of left arm and wrist staying constant throughout, with no change to the angle of elbow or wrist. A good thought when holing short putts under pressure is to think, 'Left shoulder up, ball in the cup'. The opposite tendency perhaps is, 'Right shoulder round, ball above ground'!

CROSS-HANDED PUTTING

I am surprised more golfers don't putt cross-handed, in other words with the left hand below the right. The difficulty, perhaps, is in getting to a point where you then change from cross-handed to conventional putting.

Bernhard Langer and Jeff Hawkes with cross-handed grips ideal for short and medium length putting. This grip keeps the left wrist from breaking down through impact and minimises the chance of the right shoulder coming round. Technically it makes a great deal of sense

The most common technical weakness in a putting stroke is the left hand and wrist breaking down slightly through impact. Ideally the back of the left hand should stay firm and the wrists high. Many players set up at address with quite a pronounced kink in the back of the left wrist. This is particularly likely if using a putter that is too long. That kink can very easily break down through impact, allowing the putter head to overtake the hands. The higher the left wrist is held at address, the more locked the wrist is likely to stay.

Nevertheless, the merits of putting cross-handed mean that the left hand and arm hang in a straight line without being tense. There is then far less likelihood of the left wrist breaking down through impact. The most common cross-handed grip is simply to put the left hand below the right, with no overlap, and to stretch the left index finger down the club. The left index finger is then used in moving the club back slowly, both hands being able to work the putter through, again without any tendency for the back of the left hand to give.

Another advantage of cross-handed putting is that the left hand, as well as being below the right, is now slightly ahead of the right, making it less likely for the right shoulder to work forwards. It often becomes easier with this grip for players to make a pronounced movement upwards of the left shoulder rather than forwards with the right.

Those players who do putt cross-handed usually do so only to a distance of 15 or 20 feet and from there use a conventional grip and stroke.

Particularly for the good golfer who pulls more short putts to the left than he would like, experimenting with cross-handed putting can certainly be beneficial.

HANDS AND WRISTS

With almost all aspects of golfing technique there is some great player who does not conform to the generally expounded principles! Putting is no exception. The short putting stroke of the 1980s and 1990s is seen by most as a one piece, shoulder movement, with fairly minimal – or totally eliminated – hand action. The putting stroke of the 1960s and earlier had far more variation. There were wrist putters and shoulder putters.

Two of the greatest putters of the 1960s – Billy Casper and Arnold Palmer – were hands and wrist putters. Gary Player and Lee Trevino too both employed far more hand action than is now thought correct. The exception was Bob Charles, not just for his left handedness, but as the model of a smooth shoulder stroke and the master of the long putt. There were different ways of using the hands. Palmer's way was to stand in close to the ball, lock the knees and toes inwards, immobilise the shoulders, clamp the elbows into the side and hinge from the wrists. With a short putt the wrists literally hinged under and back and then hinged forward with the left wrist breaking. The sensitivity of the hands was all-important with the body and arms staying motionless.

Billy Casper led the scoring averages in America, winning the Vardon Trophy, on five occasions. His putting was so exceptional that Ben Hogan once supposedly commented that if Casper couldn't putt he would be outside the ropes at the tournament selling hot dogs! Casper stood alarmingly close to the ball, with his left hand at times almost anchored against his left thigh. With the very short putts his stroke was similar to Palmer's, using the left wrist to push back and to hinge through. With the slightly longer putts his action was one of hingeing the club back with the left wrist, holding the hinge and then moving through with the arms. The putter head and end of the grip both seemed to move totally parallel to the ground, with an impression of the clubhead staying low to the ground beyond impact. This 'hinge and hold' feeling was perhaps more commonly used and taught than the real wrist hinge like Palmer's.

The use of the wrists will almost certainly return. Olazabal perhaps uses just a suspicion more wrist than some. Most ideas in golf turn full circle and it will no doubt become the latest and newest method of some golfing guru. It has its merits for those for whom feel is preferred to mechanics. Certainly if the shoulder stroke lacks sensitivity (and results) a hingeing action, possibly with the right index finger adding feel, is one to practise at dusk or dawn when critical eyes are focused elsewhere!

HANG THE PUTTER

In addressing the ball there should always be a little gap between the putter face and the ball. This allows the player to adjust the clubface without fear of wobbling the ball. But what should also happen, and is very crucial to good short and medium putting, is for the pre-putt routine to include a small lift where the putter is definitely lifted off the ground. It can then be set down again so that it *touches* the grass, but all the weight of the putter must hang from the arms and shoulders before the stroke takes place. Frequently players tuck the club in too close to the ball and allow the weight of the club to

At address care must be taken to ensure that the putter **hangs** from the arms and shoulders. It may touch the grass but it must be supported by you and not the ground. Holding the club fractionally off the ground encourages the smoothest of strokes for a short, fast putt

rest on the ground, or in disastrous cases almost lean on the putter. From here, the first movement is one of gathering the weight of the club with a little jerk, making it impossible to move it away with a really slow stroke.

The putter should hang from the arms and shoulders, with, say, a centimetre or half-inch gap between the putter face and the ball. This puts you in perfect control of the putter before you start the club back. Particularly on very fast greens, if you can convince yourself to play short putts with the putter held very fractionally off the ground you will find that the smooth, slow stroke becomes very much easier.

You sometimes see players sitting the club behind the ball and then lifting it over the ball and back again. This method works for them but they don't necessarily appreciate why. The reason is that it puts the player firmly in control of the putter early on. He lifts it, has control of it and puts it back behind the ball, all the time the club hanging correctly instead of any weight being lost into the ground. So the key factor at address is that *you* must support the weight of the putter and not allow the ground to support it.

For any player with a jerky or yippy stroke the advice is often to hold the putter loosely. Sadly, the more loosely you hold it the more likely you are to allow the weight to rest on the ground. This immediately means that the stroke becomes an action of gathering the weight of the putter and jerking it back. If you can ensure that the putter is firmly under your control, not resting on the ground, before the stroke starts you have far more chance of a smooth, slow stroke.

PRACTICE SWINGS – YES OR NO?

Most top-class golfers use one or more practice swings before playing a short putt. It no doubt rehearses the stroke and also settles the nerves.

But a practice swing is not always a good thing, for what a practice swing also does is to set the direction of a putt. The practice swing *must* go in the right direction. One of the commonest errors among professionals and amateurs alike is to make a practice swing which goes at the hole instead of parallel to the line of the putt. If you do this with a putt of 15 feet it possibly doesn't matter. But if you set up beside a putt of 3 or 4 feet and aim the practice swing at the hole instead of parallel to the putt, it sets you off incorrectly. Step forward to address the ball and you are likely to be aiming off to the right. Alternatively you have to turn your whole stance and body to the left to aim the putt to the hole.

If the practice swing is simply to steady the nerves or rehearse the stroke there is no harm in making the swing in a completely different direction, but never do so at the hole itself.

Remember, too, that the practice swing should never brush the ground. This is possibly more important with long putting than with short putting, but do remember that the stroke should be as close to the ground as possible without touching it.

CREATE A WINNING ROUTINE

The object of practice is to improve performance in play and under pressure. The more precise your routine and the more consistent your whole action, the more chance you have of sinking a winning putt.

There are three ways in which to tackle a short putt. I am a great believer in practising for the event. So let's assume in each case that a ball marker or coin is used, that the ball is turned round and set in exactly the same way as you do on the course, and that you then adopt your tournament routine.

The first possibility is to mark the ball, wipe it, reset it and then proceed without a practice swing. You put the putter down behind the ball, feet apart, a little lift to ensure that you have the weight of the club in your arms and shoulders and you then make your putt. That is routine number one.

The second possibility once again involves marking, cleaning and resetting the ball. You then take hold of the putter and do one or two practice swings (try to be consistent). Keep hold of the putter and, without regripping it, set it behind the ball, feet apart, a little lift and play the putt.

The third routine, once again having cleaned and reset the ball, is to do your one or two practice swings and then to let go of the putter, setting its head down behind the ball, regripping and making your putt from there.

In other words, you either do no practice swings, you do practice swings without regripping or you do practice swings and then regrip. It doesn't matter which you do providing you do the same each time. Some players find it easier not to do a practice swing, again because of the possibility of this wrongly influencing direction. Some find that keeping hold of the putter works. Curtis Strange is a good example of this. Others who adopt this procedure in practice sometimes find it difficult to stick to under pressure and can't resist regripping the putter if feeling unsettled. The third routine is possibly the most common.

Ian Woosnam winning the Masters. Ultimately major championships are won and lost on the green. Putting can account for 40 to 50 per cent of the score but rarely receives that proportion of practice

What is important is that you rehearse your routine on the practice green. I often see players spending hours hitting putts to the hole but very rarely doing what they would actually do in a tournament. At the end of a session make yourself go through the process of playing nine or perhaps 18 putts, marking the ball in precisely the same way you would normally, from between say 3 and 5 feet, and check that you really can get each one in. The usual difference between performance on the practice green and performance under pressure seems to arise from the addition of a practice swing and taking much more time.

Practise what you intend to do on the course, examine your own routine both in practice and under pressure, and ensure that the two are identical.

SHORT PUTTING EXERCISES

A player who can drive the ball on the fairway every time and hole every short putt from under 4 feet is a match for anyone.

The tendency is often to practise putts of 5 to 8 feet but to ignore the really short ones. With a putt of 3 or 4 feet you should be able to hole every one. If you miss, it is down to you. Once you move back to 5 or 6 feet even a putting machine can't hole every putt. It is simply a question of probability. By practising from 3 or 4 feet you begin to learn a lot about your putting. You can feel the contact, know whether the ball has rolled correctly and you get feedback. If you practise from 6 feet then inevitably some of the putts will miss through chance. You don't necessarily know why the ball has missed and the feedback is far less good. So concentrate on the really short one and the stroke and technique can be easily transferred to longer putts. Here, then, are some of the best exercises to perfect short putting technique.

First, simply see how many consecutive 3-foot putts you can hole. Choose a perfectly flat putt to give yourself feedback.

The second good exercise is to spread six balls round the hole and to putt from there, giving yourself different borrows to work with. Either work with the ball in the same spot each time or move it round in a circle. It is bad practice to use three or four balls 5 or 6 inches apart. The tendency here is to aim correctly with the first one and possibly move forward to the second or third with poor alignment. It becomes rather like the error of making a practice swing in the wrong direction. If you want to practise different putts, move them well away from each other to give a real change of line to the hole. Make sure you line up each putt and be fussy about getting it in the *first* time. Any idiot can do it the second or third time!

The third exercise is to narrow the hole by positioning tee pegs at the front entrance. This really does pinpoint your attention on hitting the ball into the middle of the hole.

One of the best exercises for working at a good putting stroke is to lay another club to the left of the hole so that you putt along this. You obviously have to give yourself clearance for the putter head to go through. Ideally, set the ball just behind the end of the club. This allows you to take the putter slightly back on the inside but then enables you to see whether the putter moves squarely through towards the hole. Most players will find a tendency for their putter to be dragged slightly round to the left beyond impact. Tucking the right elbow in and working with a more pronounced left shoulder up feeling will usually help to produce a better stroke. I prefer this exercise to one of making a tramline between two clubs. It is important to feel that the putter can move back slightly inside rather than developing any tendency to take it straight back or fractionally outside.

This exercise encourages a straight through, upward movement beyond impact to keep the putter square. The clubhead can move in a touch on the backswing if desired. A good thought for a straight stroke is 'left shoulder up, ball in the cup'

Another excellent exercise for developing a good stroke is to practise a push stroke. Put the ball 18 inches or 2 feet from the hole – certainly no more than that – and roll the ball into the hole with the putter head. Don't take a backswing but simply make a push stroke. This is an illegal stroke, as any experienced golfer will no doubt appreciate, but the feeling of working at this movement can help you feel the ball roll correctly. Again it puts emphasis on the left shoulder working up as you move through, keeping the left wrist firm. Not one to do just before going out to play, however, in case you leave yourself a 2-footer on the first green!

Having developed good technique from 3 or 4 feet, one of the best exercises is to work with six balls in a line, the closest 2 feet from the hole and spreading the balls out about 18 inches apart to the last one at, say, 9 or 10 feet away. As soon as you miss a putt, start again. This keeps reasonable emphasis on the short putts and puts a competitive edge and pressure on trying to complete the whole row. One of the key benefits of this exercise is that it trains you to watch the ball long enough. With the short putts you can see the ball and see the hole out of the corner of your left eye. As you start moving back through the longer putts you get to a point where you can't see the ball go in the hole. The feeling, however, should still be one of keeping the head perfectly still and *listening* for the ball to go in.

WATCHING THE BALL

More putts under pressure are probably missed through the player looking up fractionally early than for any other reason. Practising the very short putt of 3 or 4 feet also helps in learning to keep the head still. You can see the ball and the hole at the same time; by keeping the head perfectly still and the eyes focused on the ground you still see the ball going in from the corner of your left eye. You can transfer this learning to the slightly longer putt.

The danger of practising from 6 or 7 feet, and ignoring the short ones, is that you are constantly tending to look up to see where the ball goes; head movement becomes part of your action and is more likely to creep in with the occasional 3-footer.

Possibly the best exercise – and it is only an exercise – is to practise putting with a ball marker or a coin behind the ball. The feeling is very definitely of looking at the ball marker after the ball has gone, thus training yourself to keep your eyes still and to see the ball out of the corner of your left eye. Most golfers, including many very good ones, move their head or eyes more than they imagine.

The exercise is particularly good using a coin. Put the putter down on top of the coin, leaving a gap between the putter face and the ball, and holding the putter fractionally off the coin at address. Again it gives the feeling of the club *hanging* from the arms and shoulders and not resting on the ground.

Some professional golfers prefer to look at the ground rather than the ball with a short putt. By focusing on the grass rather than the ball they find it easier to keep the head still and the eyes from wandering. The danger, of course, is that if your eyes move your head starts moving and so, under pressure, do the shoulders. The usual result is the putter pulling away to the left. Under pressure the head and eyes must stay still but without freezing and thus losing the feeling of the left shoulder working upwards.

EVERY PUTT IS A STRAIGHT PUTT

The key to good sidehill putting is to remember that every putt is a straight putt. In other words, you have to choose a line and make a good stroke to the spot you have chosen. Particularly on a right-to-left putt, players will often lose the feeling of a straight stroke and start swinging the putter round in a slight curve, if anything dragging the putter to the left. The feeling must be of choosing a precise spot, going through your routine and making the putt to that spot without the stroke deteriorating.

LEFT: One of the real keys to good short putting is to hit the ball from the sweetspot of the club. More short putts are probably missed by pros from striking the ball fractionally in the heel than for any other reason. On a left to right putt, however, striking the ball closer to the heel keeps the ball up to the left

Some players definitely prefer a right-to-left putt and others a left-to-right putt. On any short putt it is important to hit the ball on the right part of the clubface, preferably from the exact sweet spot. If you hit the ball slightly in the heel the ball can spin away to the left, and if you hit it slightly towards the toe it can spin away to the right. The danger on a right-to-left putt is of hitting the ball fractionally towards the heel. The ball simply won't hold its line and drops away to the left prematurely. On a right-to-left putt, strike the ball a touch more towards the toe to help hold the ball up the slope. Hitting the putt fractionally heelside of centre is a common cause for a slightly mis-hit, inaccurate short putt. So a right-to-left putt needs particular care.

Conversely, on a left-to-right putt, striking the ball fractionally towards the heel will keep the ball up to the left, any tendency towards striking it from the toe allowing it to spin away. A good strike on the ball is vital with both sidehill putts.

On the right-to-left putt the usual danger is of the stroke becoming a curve rather than a straight line. The same pattern follows as with the long game, though of course the differences are now minute. In standing even fractionally below the ball your head and eyes may not be truly over it, the hands may sit slightly lower and the whole tendency can be to swing the club round in a little more of a curve. Having the feet an inch or two below the ball is also likely to throw you slightly further away from it, just as with

RIGHT: With a right to left putt the ball tends to be dragged left just as it does on a long, sidehill shot. In the stroke keep the ball a touch nearer the toe, stand tall to counteract the slope and ensure that the stroke is a straight stroke to the chosen spot and doesn't deteriorate into a curved path

a full shot from a side slope. It is important to stand in close enough to the ball, standing tall and counteracting the lie of the land.

On a very sloping short putt we not only have to get the line but also the length. It is no good the ball breaking, for example, from right-to-left but breaking 3 inches before it should or 3 inches too late. A good concept is to imagine that the putt is two straight lines. You start the ball on one line towards a definite spot and from there it turns down the hill towards the hole. This is likely to produce a better stroke than seeing it as a curve. The skill is of hitting the ball just the right length so that it takes up its break correctly. An excellent exercise on a flat green is to putt to a ball marker set totally flush into the green. The feeling is of trying to stop the ball on the marker. It is easy to think only of direction with short putts and ignore distance. In this way you learn to get control over the strength of the putt. Now the feeling on the sidehill lie is of choosing the spot, imagining you putt the ball precisely to the spot and from there allowing it to turn down towards the hole.

SPEED AND THE SHORT PUTT

On a short sidehill putt on a quick green you can't determine the precise line without knowing how hard the player intends to hit the ball. Players like Tom Watson almost straighten out the borrow of a sidehill putt by hitting the ball firmly at the side or the back of the hole. Providing it hits the centre of the hole, the ball drops. If it misses it will go several feet past. Another player will play the putt far more cautiously and have to allow for far more side slope.

What is important is that you practise putts with the same speed as you use on the course. Many players practise their putting from 4 or 5 feet, hitting the ball far harder on the practice green than they do on the course. Without contemplating what happens if the ball misses, the player uses a quite aggressive stroke. The ball holds its line well, hits the back of the hole and drops in. The same player on the golf course may use a far more cautious approach, the ball travelling more slowly and not, of course, holding its line as well.

We must practise for play and for pressure. For this reason, as well as practising on a flat lie you must also practise sidehill putts. Each one needs to be tackled with concentration. Put yourself under pressure. 'This putt to win the British Open.' Make yourself do it correctly each time, as though in the actual situation.

Some players are aggressive short putters, others fairly cautious. Remember that a ball travelling too slowly won't hold its line. A good exercise for the player who under-hits short putts and tends to trickle them in is to put a tee peg or ball marker in the back of the hole and to practise short putts, making sure that the ball really does hit the back of the hole before dropping. The other school of thought is that a dying putt has more chance of creeping in the side door. The line, however, is far more sensitive.

WHY DO WE THREE PUTT?

The most common reason for three putting is an error of distance and *not* an error of direction. It is only on a very sloping green that the low-handicap golfer is likely to misread a green or mis-hit the ball to such an extent that he leaves the ball 3 feet or more wide of the hole. No, three putts almost always come from distance errors. Just think how often you attend a flag for a player who hits what looks a good putt and you find yourself saying, 'Oh, good putt, good putt', only to see the ball miss the hole by 2 or 3 inches and then go 6 or 7 feet past. Equally, it rolls down on line towards you and then stops 4 feet short. It is not often that you see a real error of direction which leaves the player struggling to get down in two.

The problem is that we *see* directional errors far more than we see distance errors. A ball travelling 12 inches to the side of the hole, from 8 or 10 paces, leaves the player feeling disgusted. Hit a putt bang on line and it looks good. But you can have considerable difficulty in stopping it within 12 inches lengthwise.

Most players seem to put 90 per cent of their thoughts with a medium or long putt into the line and ignore the distance. If on the other hand you become good at judging length, you become a reliable medium and long putter; simply by the law of averages a reasonable number will drop in. Even with a putt of, say, 12 to 15 feet the distance becomes far more difficult to judge than the direction.

I use one particular exercise for medium putting with all my players from rabbit to national champion. Choose a putt of six paces, preferably downhill, and mark off a box with four tee pegs beyond the hole. The box should be one putter's length in both width and depth but starting 3 inches beyond the hole. Now take six balls from six paces. Give yourself two points if you get the ball in the hole and one if you get it in the box. It sounds very easy but in fact can be extremely difficult. Most amateur golfers initially leave the ball short of the hole. The medium-handicap player who leaves it 6 or 9 inches short usually thinks the putt is good, but in reality the ball has no chance of going in. He then starts attacking the hole to get in the box and finishes going out of the box on the other side. It is very unusual to find even a scratch golfer who finds it easy to get all six balls in either the hole or the box.

What we do notice from this exercise, however, is that nobody, however long a handicap, ever has difficulty in the direction of the box! Even the very worst of putts would finish in the box for direction but relatively few do for distance. If you hit six balls the right length, by the law of averages one, two or three will drop. The same thing follows on the golf course. If you consistently hit the ball the right length, some go in. Even a putting machine can't get six balls in the hole from this distance; there is always an element of chance.

Some players curse their bad luck with medium-length putts. The ball rolls towards the hole and then, just as it is getting there, turns off-line. The player usually blames the greenkeeper for not changing the hole correctly! The real reason is that the ball isn't travelling firmly enough to hold its line.

A ball first slides, then rolls, then takes up wobble. In the last few inches the ball can potentially wobble off-line. Even on the most perfect green, a ball usually rolls over and over and then, as it comes to rest, simply turns slightly one way or the other. If travelling too slowly, it almost reaches the hole and then just won't drop. That is why the box of pegs starts 3 or 4 inches beyond the hole. The ball that doesn't reach the box is often just slightly under-hit. On the course it could easily lose its line and with it the accuracy to drop. The perfect speed for any putt is one that would travel 6 to 9 inches beyond the hole, whether uphill or downhill and whatever the length.

LONG PUTTING – PRACTICE SWINGS AND THE STRIKE

The key to good long putting is judgement of distance, which comes from rolling the ball with a consistent strike. With medium-length putts of, say, 5 to 10 paces, the technique can be relatively unimportant. Some players begin to stand further away from the ball, drop their hands slightly and may not necessarily watch the ball terribly well. It is all about feel. But with long putting, technique

Three putting is usually from poor length, not poor line. Distance is far harder to judge than direction. Practise hitting 6 balls from 6 paces. Give yourself 2 points for each that is holed and 1 point for each finishing within a putter length past the hole. Once this distance is mastered, particularly downhill, work at the same routine for longer putts

again becomes important. It is essential to strike the ball well and consistently.

As a first key to long putting, make sure the stroke is long enough. Sometimes we see medium- and long-handicap golfers with an overly long stroke. But as a rule with low-handicap players the tendency is to make too short a swing, the player then having to accelerate unnecessarily through impact. The feeling of the stroke should be of a long, slow one. Always have two or three practice swings with a long putt, making sure that the practice swing is the same length you will use with the ball and, very importantly, that the practice swing doesn't brush the ground. If the practice swing does brush the ground, the depth and strike on the ball become inconsistent. You want the putter travelling as close to the ground as possible without actually scuffing it.

Some players like to make the stroke with their shoulders, some with their arms and others with their hands. It doesn't matter providing the stroke is consistent, the ball is struck from the middle of the clubface and the depth is good.

Nick Price, the 1994 Open Champion, thanks in part to a superbly judged 20 yard eagle putt on the penultimate hole

The key thing to practise is the feeling of being able to roll the ball the right length. It is easy to become so obsessed with the line that you forget the length. It is far more difficult with a long putt to get the ball within 3 feet for distance than 1 foot for direction. The pros' choice of the world's best long putter is Ben Crenshaw. Ben always says he never tries to hole a long putt, just to hit it the right length and into a 3-foot circle round the hole.

There are several exercises to help good long putting. The first one is to take a piece of string, peg it down on the green and practise putting your ball so that it just crosses the string. Another is to putt towards the hole, setting out a row of teepegs 3 feet beyond the hole. See just how many putts you can make finish between the hole and the string. Work over and over again from different distances from 5 paces up to 20 paces, constantly thinking of the strike and the roll. Make sure that you watch the ball long enough and hit it accurately from the middle of the clubface.

THE THREE-BALL EXERCISE

One way of improving long putting is to focus your attention on the contact with the ball. Any tendency to look away early can easily produce a very slightly mis-hit putt that doesn't roll the right length. The feeling should be of your head staying still and your eyes looking down at the ground until the ball is at least half way there. This means that under pressure there is some room for deterioration without actually looking up too soon.

In this exercise take three balls, all identical but preferably with different numbers. Hit them in number order. Putt the first ball down the green, feeling the way you strike it. Then, without following it with your eyes, strike ball number two, feeling the strike and trying to make it go the same length. Follow with number three, again without watching it. If your strike is consistent all three balls should finish close to each other, say within 18 inches. If your strike is inconsistent you can usually begin to feel which one is wrong. It makes you more aware of the clubface on the ball.

Very often you will find you can put three balls closer together feeling the strike than by using your eyes and watching each one. By concentration on the *feel* of the clubface striking the ball, the accuracy of strike is better and the roll of the ball begins to improve.

LONG PUTTING – STARTING THE BALL STRAIGHT

Good golfers faced with a long, straight putt would have very little difficulty hitting the ball within several inches of the hole widthways. The problem for some starts as soon as they allow for any borrow. Very often the player will look at a line, choose a spot, say, 18 inches to the left of the hole and then fail to start the ball accurately. He may choose a spot and then over-borrow, starting the ball a lot further to the side than he means.

Again, as with the short putt we need to see every putt as a straight putt. We choose a spot, whether well short of the hole and to the side, or level with the hole and to the side, and should then play the ball straight to that spot. If you start seeing the putt as a curve it is easy to over-borrow or alternatively to start the ball where you mean but to allow the stroke to deteriorate into a ragged curve.

Remember that you can always ask the person attending the flag to stand on one side of the hole or the other. As a rule it is far easier to have him standing on the high side of the hole and feel you can aim towards his feet than to have him stand on the low side of the hole. It tends to focus your attention and make judgement of the line easier.

READING THE GREEN

The first key to reading greens is to get a feeling for the overall slope. Unless the green is very undulating, the golden rule is that the majority of putts will go with the overall slope. (For the moment we will ignore the question of grain and special conditions.)

Remember that on the majority of golf courses built within the last 40 or 50 years the general principle is that players want to land the ball on the green and see it stop. The back of the green tends to be built higher than the front. On the other hand, at old fashioned championship courses built more than 50 years ago, the rule is often exactly the opposite. The thought at that time was that you should never build the back of the green higher than the front because it gave the player confidence! For this reason, on many old championship courses you find the back of the green lower than the front, making it extremely difficult to stop the ball.

We need to understand the overall slope. Remember that it is very easy to see upslope but extremely difficult to see downslope. If you walk onto a green where the back is higher than the front it is quite obvious. But if you walk onto a green which looks flat, the back of the green may be lower than the front and the downslope eluding you. You will often hear people play a putt, see the ball whistle past the hole and then say, 'Oh, I didn't realise it was downhill.' You never hear anyone say he didn't realise a putt was uphill! He might not realise how much uphill it is but will at least see an upslope.

One of golf's great double acts. Looking from right down low sees the minutest of imperfections but can lose the overall feeling for the slope of the green. Taking a higher view keeps the overall lie of the land in mind

Determine which is the lowest part of the green and to read a medium or long putt simply use this information. Supposing we have a green that tips down from back to front. Any putt on the right of the green is a right-to-left putt and any putt on the left of the green a left-to-right putt. Everything breaks from the back of the green. It is worth positioning golf balls 6 or 8 paces from the hole round in a circle. From the right of the green we have a very definite right-to-left putt. As we work round the back of the green it becomes a left-to-right putt. The key area is the part where we are getting almost directly above the hole. Are we still in the area of a right-to-left putt, have we come to the top of the slope where the ball is run-ning straight down or have we passed this point and do we now have a left-to-right putt? It is this area of the green where the putts are most complex. On the others we may not allow the right amount of borrow but at least we know we are faced with a right-to-left putt. The danger is of getting to this particular zone and starting to read the putt wrongly. We begin looking at it as a left-to-right putt when in fact it is a right-to-left putt. The golden rule at this point has to be, 'If in doubt, hit it straight.' Particularly with medium and long putts, these are the ones most likely to cause trouble. Once the ball takes up the break it begins to run downhill and if running the wrong way can show quite an error. When you get the corresponding zone from below the hole, if you do aim to the wrong side at least the ball doesn't take up as much speed on the wrong line.

The key point is to work on the principle of putts always following the overall slope. Very often you will read a putt better by standing slightly away from the ball and looking at it from above than by getting down too close. It is easy to get down so close to the ball and to focus on such a small area of the green that you lose this overall slope and make a quite drastic error. Certainly, on a very perfect tournament prepared course the minutest imperfection in the green can have a bearing. But remember that the ball is at it most susceptible in the last yard of the putt. At this point the ball is slowing down and imperfections and tiny borrows have more effect. This area may need very careful thought, but remember all the time that from 6 paces and beyond it is still the distance which is far more likely to be a problem than the line.

If you walk onto a green that appears flat, particularly if the fairway has been downhill, then do make sure that you really know how the green slopes. Try to get a view of the green from behind and make a clear judgement of the overall fall. The greens that cause the most problems on any course are the ones that slope from front down to back. Players not only misread the speed of a ball from the front of the green, but also often borrow completely the wrong side on putts from the side of the green. Remember that the older the course the more likely you are to find downhill greens, and always be prepared for the difficulty of the unexpected, unseen, downhill putt.

READING GREENS – WIND AND GRAIN

Most golfers make insufficient allowance for the way the wind can affect a putt. On a seaside course the wind can have a very definite influence on the speed of the putt. Putting into the wind or downwind needs very careful consideration; it has far more effect than most people imagine. If you have a downhill, downwind putt it needs the gentlest of touches. Hit a ball into the wind, particularly uphill, and you really do have to take it into account. In windy conditions always have the flag held initially with the material flapping, to get a feeling for the wind speed and direction. Remember, too, that on a sidehill putt where you expect the ball to turn into the wind, the wind can very easily keep it out.

Another point to consider is the grain of the grass. On most courses in the British Isles, grain isn't a particular problem. The effect, for those who don't understand it, is like the lines made with a cylinder mower. As the mower cuts in a direction away from you, the grass is pushed down and it will seem shiny. As the mower runs towards you, so the grass grows towards you and the stripe appears darker.

In many hot countries, however, the grass will grow with a definite grain that can be of almost more effect than the slope. Sometimes it grows towards the setting sun, while on other courses it will grow towards a supply of water. In Japan there are courses where the grass simply grows in the direction in which everyone walks. In some areas the grass will very definitely grow away from a mountain or towards the sea. Don't ignore the growth of the grass. You can partly see the grain by looking at the dark and shiny effect, but you should also trust any overall rule proffered by local caddies. Allowing for the grain is basically like allowing for the slope. If you are putting across the grain the ball will run with it and may well run slightly uphill. A putt downhill, down-grain can be extraordinarily fast. If putting into a heavy grain the effect can literally be so strong that you can hear the ball moving through the grass. You have to experience it to believe it!

Sometimes the problem is one of assessing the overall direction of the grain. You are obviously not allowed to wipe your hands or club across the grass to test the grain in play, but it is well worth doing so in practice. Sometimes the grass just off the side of the green, being that much longer, can give good guidance. It is also worth looking at the way the cup is cut. With a strong grain you can actually see the blades of grass slightly hanging over one side of the hole and growing away from the other. This is often the case when the grass grows towards the sun. Leave the ball on the lip of the hole, going with the grain, put the ball in shadow so that the grass settles towards the sun, and the ball drops in! Maybe not in accordance with the rules, but it demonstrates just how strong the effect of grain can be. The key factor for those not used to it is to understand that the effect of grain has to be taken into account and to learn from the locals.

There, then, are some ideas on the art of putting. Remember that putts account for some 40 to 50 per cent of the scratch golfer's shots. They rarely receive 40 to 50 per cent of the practice time and thought!

Jack Nicklaus – the golfer who has holed more pressure putts to win major championships than any other player

8

THE SHORT GAME

CHIPPING

With the ball just off the side of the green the first choice should simply be to putt the ball; but a short chip for a very good player can often be more accurate. Starting the ball, even for a very short distance, through the air can often be more predictable than a ball travelling across a less than perfect surface. Let's initially consider a tiny shot with a 6- or 7-iron.

Sam Torrance with the typical tournament player's chipping action – reverse overlap putting grip, left elbow dropped well into the side

The key point with the chip is to stand in close enough to the ball, preferably gripping it in the same way you grip your putter. A tall player will usually find chipping relatively easy, being able to stand in close with his eyes over the ball. Somebody smaller will usually get too far away from the ball without getting the eyes on line. To produce the correct address position sit the club slightly on its toe (as a starting point so that you can read the writing on the top of the grip) and hold the club in exactly the same way as you would your putter. Preferably use the reverse overlap grip, left index finger out. Grip your putter, seeing how far your hands are from the ground, and then find the same sort of height and length with the 7-iron. For most people this will bring the right index finger down to the end of the grip. The club should preferably sit at much the same lie as the putter, making the two shots feel as similar as possible.

The benefit of the reverse overlap grip is that it weakens the left hand. In other words, the left hand is taken round to the left on the shaft, and the left elbow sits into the side, almost on the left hip. As the right hand is added, we should once again see the heel of the right hand sitting *against* the middle finger of the left hand. Once more, keep a definite space in the

palm of the right hand rather than slotting the left thumb into it. The hands are now in a much more open position than they would be with the long game. But the key is the left hand. To get the right feeling it is worth repeating the same exercise as with the putter, holding the club out in front of you at waist height, elbows slightly into the side, arching the wrists up and tipping the club over. From here, bend over to take up your address position, feeling that the club is sitting up towards its toe. The top of the shaft points up towards you rather than sticking back into you. Looking at the writing on, or hole in, the top of the grip is a good starting point. This is slightly exaggerated but it does give the right feeling.

Another way of finding the correct position is to take hold of the club with your right thumb and index finger, hang it vertically so that it sits on its toe, stand perhaps 9 or 10 inches away from the ball and then ease the top of the club back until you can take hold of it with your putting grip. With the club held in this way, slightly on its toe, the ball should also be played slightly towards the toe. We don't want the strength and power of the middle of the club. By striking the ball more towards the toe you get a

The short chip with a 7-iron. The club is gripped with a putting grip, the left hand weak enough round to the left to allow the left elbow to sit in on the hip, hands well down the shaft, weight slightly on the left foot. The putting grip allows a little use of the hands for feel, without allowing the wrists to take over

much softer, more delicate feeling, particularly from a heavy fringe onto a quick green.

The position of the left hand and arm is very important. The top of the club should be sitting inside the left forearm. As you swing the club back, if there is any wrist action at all – and it doesn't matter if there is – the top of the club will just catch the inside of the forearm, limiting this wrist action. As the stroke is taken on through, the back of the left hand stays firm. From this address position the advanced golfer can use a little bit of hand action in the backswing without being afraid of it. If by contrast the left-hand grip is strong, the top of the club can very easily be allowed to pass *under* the left forearm, permitting too large a backswing, with the wrist action becoming too active. Tucking the left elbow in and weakening the left hand produces control.

The 7-iron is brought up to the lie of a putter, sitting up on its toe. With the left elbow in, the top of the club sits in against the inside of the left wrist. In the backswing the top of the club just eases back to touch the inside of the wrist, limiting the hand action but allowing just a little. The ball is struck towards the toe for a short chip to deaden the speed and to reduce the drag through thick grass

The good golfer is unlikely to release too early with the wrists in the throughswing. It is as though the wrists can just do a tiny bit in the backswing and the wrist action is then held as the club moves through. Certainly the shot will have a little more hand action than the putting stroke and the club does, if anything, brush the ground. But otherwise the feeling should be as close to putting as possible. With medium- and higher-handicap golfers, the fault is often to release with the wrists in the throughswing. An exercise I use here is to place a cotton reel between the top of the club and the inside of the player's left forearm, making him chip while trapping the reel in position. It stops any feeling of releasing with the wrists. For the good golfer it ensures that the end of the club and the forearm stay together, without any tendency to arch the left wrist and let the club shaft work beneath it.

The ball can be positioned fairly centrally in the stance, as long as the weight is slightly ahead of it. The contact should be clean, just brushing the ground without any tendency to hit the ball on the downswing. Striking the ball slightly towards the toe of the club gives a nice, gentle feeling and takes away the tendency for many players of being slightly heavy-handed. Once again, as with long putting, distance rather than direction is the real key. Accuracy of strike from the right part of the clubface is all-important.

For those who can chip well, the accuracy of distance judgement, particularly for a downhill shot, is often better than in putting. The backspin of any chip, even a relatively low one, gives a better braking system than the initial sliding effect of a putt.

CHIPPING FROM THE TOE

There are two real reasons for striking the ball towards the toe of the club with a short chip. Firstly, the club should be sitting slightly on its toe to enable you to get your eyes over the ball. This is more apparent the shorter the player and the flatter the lie of the club. Secondly, striking the ball towards the toe also weakens the feeling of the strike. This allows the shot to be judged more delicately. Certainly up to a distance of 10 yards or so, particularly where the green is fast, this will give a very sensitive touch.

Another reason for playing the ball towards the toe is where the fringe around the green is heavy and well watered. The grass may have a definite grain and produce resistance. By sitting the club on its toe there is far less drag. The toe of the club can more easily work through the grass than with the club sitting flat. The closer you can convince yourself to stand with the shots, the left hand in a weak position, left elbow in, the better the contact you can make.

A good exercise to force yourself to play the ball from the toe is to set up a row of balls with no more than half an inch between them. This forces you to play the ball towards the toe to get the shots away cleanly one at a time.

Another excellent exercise for learning to chip really delicately is to practise on a green. If played correctly, the shot never causes any damage. Line up a row of balls, the closest, say, 3 feet from the hole, spreading them 2 feet apart or so, and preferably working with a downhill or slightly side-hill shot – definitely not uphill. Set up to the shots, holding the 6- or 7-iron as if it were a putter. Play the ball from towards the toe and imagine you are putting it. The closest one or two may not seem to lift; but from there you will detect the minutest backspin and begin to feel perfect control.

THE LEFT HAND AND ARM

The most common bad chipping action, particularly among lowish-handicap golfers, is of having the left arm too straight, the left hand in too strong a grip position, and allowing the hands to produce too much potential power in the backswing. In the *wrong* address position the top of the club can pass *under* the left arm, often producing erratic distance.

Having learnt to weaken the left hand and to tuck the left elbow in, the player can usually find the feeling of sitting the club up on the toe when playing from thickish grass. But the difficulty then often arises when chipping from a tighter lie.

Wrong. If the left arm is straight and the wrists dropped the club shaft can wrongly work under the left arm, allowing the action to become loose. An ordinary golf grip with the left hand too strong allows this; the weaker left hand of the putter grip avoids it

It is essential from a tighter lie to be able to get the club sitting flatter on its bottom while still keeping a weakish left hand and the left elbow in. There are many shots around the green that need this same kind of position, whether or not with the putting grip. So, from a tighter lie, the feeling can be of standing a little further from the ball, having the club sitting flatter to the ground, tucking the left elbow into the side and again with a sense that the top of the club is close to the left forearm. It is as though there is a straight line from the left elbow to the clubhead. The feeling should not be of hanging the left arm straight and having the angle of the club shaft below this. From this correct position, wrist action is again limited. The hands can be just that little bit active on the backswing, encouraging really good feel, without the danger of their taking over or the action becoming wristy.

VARYING LENGTHS WITH CHIPPING

The easiest way of altering the length of a chip, when we want more roll, is simply to change the angle of the clubface rather than chopping and changing clubs. Most players seem to do better by working with a 6- or 7-iron and getting used to adapting it rather than working with the 7 down to the 4. In order to lengthen the chip, the feeling can simply be of shutting the clubface down a touch – again using the putting grip – playing the ball a tiny bit further back in the stance and allowing the weight to be ahead of the ball.

To adjust the loft of the club, always hold it in the right hand first and then set the club to the loft you require. From here, adjust your foot position, moving ahead of the ball as necessary, and lean a touch to the left so that the end of the club shaft always points towards your belly button or just a shade left of it. Then add the left hand. Feel the toes and knees turned a touch towards the target. When manoeuvring the clubhead to a different loft, always do so with the right hand first. Then adjust feet and weight.

At a certain distance there is no longer any need to have the club sitting on the toe (unless the grass is very fluffy), nor to have the ball towards the toe. The club can sit fairly flat to the ground but still with the left hand in a weak position, left elbow into the side. As the length of the shot increases, so the body will begin to move a shade further to the left. The golden rule, with these as with almost all short shots, is to keep the right shoulder relatively high. As the chip lengthens, make sure there is no tendency to let the right shoulder drop. By the time you are playing a chip of 20 or 30 yards, the top half of the body should be allowed to move through slightly, your eyes staying focused on the ball well through impact but your head possibly moving a couple of inches to the left.

Rather than thinking of where the ball lands, the best way of judging distance is simply by thinking of the overall length of the shot, getting the ball down on the ground relatively quickly and running it the rest of the way. Once again it is the distance that is all important. Direction is unlikely to be a problem.

By the time you get to a running shot of 40 or 50 yards you may still like the feeling of a putting grip or you may prefer your ordinary golf grip. Whichever grip you use, the left arm should still stay in its very passive position at address. The feeling now must be of maintaining a wide enough stance to allow a little weight to transfer. Turning both feet slightly towards the target may also help in weight transference. The feeling should be that the top half of the body moves through with the right shoulder staying high. Your head will start opposite the ball. By the time you finish, your head will have moved 2 or 3 inches to the left. Feel that you can still look down at the ground long enough, but allow the top half to move through. The most common fault for the good player is of allowing the right side to drop instead of keeping the right shoulder up.

CHIPPING AND SHORT PITCHING

The other variation in choice of clubs comes as we move further from the green, with some fluffy grass to negotiate. On many courses with very heavy aprons this means choosing a club where you can pitch the ball onto the green. On a typical British seaside or heathland course it is perfectly possible to run the ball through the apron and there is no need to take a lofted club.

As soon as you need more carry and less run, the choice obviously has to be of a more lofted club. This may mean using the 8, 9, pitching wedge or sand wedge in exactly the same way as the 6- or 7-iron. Using the reverse overlap putting grip adds feel and delicacy to the shot. The clubs naturally sit more upright and are slightly shorter, and, although the same principles of grip and stance follow, there may be less feeling of having to sit the club slightly on the toe. The set of clubs does this for you. But still very important is to keep the left elbow relaxed, to stay in close to the ball with your eyes predominantly over it, and to make a swing where the back of the left hand stays firm.

Having chosen the correct club to carry you onto the green, the easiest way of judging length for most players is to look at overall length rather than simply thinking of where the ball will land. If you concentrate too much on the landing spot it is easy firstly, to choose one too short and, secondly, to land short of this anyway. By looking at the overall length, most players find it easier to get the ball to the hole and preferably past it.

The feeling of the contact should be fairly clean, just brushing the ground on which the ball sits, without any ball-divot contact.

With a very tiny chip with a pitching wedge or sand wedge the danger can be of striking the ball twice, the clubhead catching up with the ball

The shorter the pitch the more difficult many players find it. The putting grip can be used to control the wrists and clubhead speed. Wrist action should be kept to a minimum. The top of the club points to your belly button at address and points to it all the way. In the throughswing the back of the left wrist must stay firm, arching up rather than breaking down

again. The feeling should always be of just sliding the clubhead away a little to the left, thus removing the danger.

Modern championship courses are usually set up with extremely fluffy fringes and very quick greens. From certain positions at the back of the green you have to pitch the ball just a yard or so with a pitching wedge or sand wedge, from the heaviest of fringes, onto a very quick green. It is essential here for the back of the left wrist to be completely firm and for the club to move smoothly through impact – not rushing or the club grabs it, not decelerating or the shot is fluffed. In this position, in particular, use of the reverse overlap grip adds strength and control to the left hand. The left elbow stays in, left arm shortening away, and at the end of the shot the butt end of the grip should seem to lock in against the inside of the left wrist or forearm.

SHORT PITCHING

A short pitch of 5 to 10 yards over a bunker is usually far more difficult for most players than the longer one. Many players easily hit a shot of 25 or 30 yards but find the short ones difficult, usually because of using too much hand action.

As a starting point it is important to get a good sand iron to pitch with round the greens. The difference between a sand iron and a pitching wedge is quite dramatic. If you take a worm's eye view along the bottom of a sand iron the lowest point is the back or middle of the flange. The front edge would naturally sit slightly off the ground. By contrast, the lowest point on the sole of a pitching wedge is its leading edge, giving it a cutting edge. The sand iron is made to bounce and the pitching wedge to cut. In playing shots around the green the sand wedge is far more commonly used by professionals, who will usually use a pitching wedge only with chipping or for uphill lies.

The key factor with the short pitch is to minimise wrist action. An excellent way of feeling this is again to use the reverse overlap putting grip, practising some short pitches from a very slight upslope. If you can find a bank at the back of a green, then just work with the ball 12 or 18 inches over the top of the bank; this is a great position for learning the short pitch. The slight upslope gives you the feeling of elevation, and also encourages you to lean into it while giving the correct feeling of the movement beyond impact.

In most shots around the green the left arm is always kept in and relaxed throughout the shot, left wrist firm. The other golden rule of the short game is that the right shoulder stays high for a steeper attack and never drops down and under

The shorter shaft of the sand iron should automatically bring you in close enough to the ball, eyes reasonably well over it. The key point to develop is firmness of the back of the left hand through and beyond impact. Remember with every golf shot we play that the left arm has to shorten away beyond impact. In this case the left elbow will break slightly in and behind you with the back of the left wrist staying firm and uppermost. The clubface, too, should look upwards as it moves beyond impact. The danger with these shots is that players, often good with their hands in the long game, start using their wrists through impact. Instead of the clubface coming through into a *face up* position, left elbow breaking away behind you, the wristy player will often let the clubhead pass the hands, almost as though closing it through impact, producing too much speed.

Having learnt the feeling from a slight upslope, the feeling from an ordinary, grassy lie for a shot of 10 yards or so is precisely the same. The back of the left hand should stay perfectly firm as you move on through impact, left elbow if anything shortening and breaking away behind you. A good exercise is to have a few practice swings with the right hand only. At the finish add the left hand, feeling the small space into which the left arm fits. The arm relaxes and shortens; the wrist stays firm.

THE SHORT GAME 149

SHORT PITCHING – ELIMINATING THE WRISTS

In playing a short pitch with a sand iron, the wrist action should be kept to a minimum. In the basic short pitch from a good lie, keep the club shaft pointing straight up towards your belly button, giving yourself the full loft on the club. The feeling should be of using the arms and shoulders, and possibly some leg action, with no wrist action. Imagine the club shaft pointing up towards you. As you swing back and through, the end of the club should feel to stay pointing to your belly button throughout, with no wrist action. If there is any breaking of the wrists in the backswing, too much potential power is created, often producing deceleration in the downswing. A good exercise for feeling the short pitch, particularly for the longer-handicap player, is to hold the end of the club into your belly button, arms extended down the shaft, and to make a few practice swings well above the ground, feeling the club shaft locked into position. This cuts out any wrist action and puts emphasis on the shoulders and legs.

For an advanced player an excellent way of feeling the right action is to make two or three practice swings watching the grip end of the club. If you play the shot without any wrist action, the end of the club stays visible all the time. If, by contrast, you allow yourself to use your hands, the top of the club disappears behind the left forearm on the backswing.

In playing the shot, particularly from a good lie, allow the club shaft to sit directly up towards you. Make a couple of practice swings, rehearsing the action and the depth, and then play the shot keeping the wrists firm, if anything allowing the left elbow to shorten away behind you in the end of the stroke. Make sure, however, that the back of the left hand is always uppermost in the finish, clubface upwards and never turning into a toe-up position.

In this way, plenty of height to the shot is produced without any feeling of having to help the ball up with the hands.

SHORT PITCHES FROM A TIGHT LIE

The good player will usually find a short pitch from a good lie relatively easy. The problems begin when the lie is tighter. The first consideration is the sort of soil you are playing from. From a predominantly sandy type of soil, even if the lie looks very tight, there is usually enough give in the ground to be able to play the shot in the normal way. If on the other hand the ground is wet or the lie is rock hard, we have to make adjustments.

From a tight lie, first see if there is any give in the ground. Start in exactly the same address position as from a good lie, without pressing the hands forward to the left. Allow the club to sit naturally on its flange without worrying if the front edge is fractionally off the ground. Make two or three practice swings, again with no wrist action but feeling as if you are holding the flange of the club *down* into the ground as though bouncing it through. The flange of the club should simply *dent* the ground, allowing

you to feel that you can find the bottom of the ball. The little mark that you see on the ground is not a divot but simply a little dent. Set up to the ball, think almost entirely of the depth of your contact, push the flange down into the ground as you make contact with ground and ball and you should easily make good depth and a good strike. It is really a question of knowing your own sand iron, of feeling that you can hold the club down into the ground and still find the bottom of the ball from this kind of lie.

If by contrast you are playing on hard ground which is clay or chalk, there may be no give in it. As the flange of the club makes contact with the ground, it seems to bounce up; the feeling is that you can't find the bottom of the ball. Have a couple of practice swings to experiment. If this is the case, the club needs to be set up differently so that it sits on its front edge. Take hold of the club, tip it forward a touch and make sure the front edge is on the ground. The golden rule with these shots is that the club shaft is going to point roughly to your belly button as opposed to your left shoulder. Therefore, with the club in this new position, simply stand a little ahead of the ball. Set the club to the ball and experiment with the feeling you need. Then move away from it and have a couple of practice swings. In this case the contact will feel as though it needs to be a ball-divot contact.

To produce the ball-divot contact we need not just a curve through impact but the feeling of a curve, a little straight line where we get the

To play a short, high pitch, the wrists are dropped low at address. This low wrist position gives the impression of an early wrist break in the back swing. In reality the wrist angle is all created at address and held firmly from start to finish

divot and then out again on another curve. To produce this, the feeling must be of the top half of your body moving forwards. Imagine that the club comes down, your head moves to the left to correspond with taking the divot, and the club comes out and up again. In this shot the top half must be allowed to move through just fractionally to produce the correct ball-divot contact. The right shoulder must stay high as the top half moves. Your head starts opposite the ball; it finishes opposite your left foot, but all the time you are watching the ball well to make the slight ball-divot contact.

Exactly the same contact is required with the ball on a slightly wet lie. You don't want the feeling of the club catching the ground before or beneath the ball, but you do want a ball-divot contact. Once again the club should sit on its front edge. The hands will naturally be a little more ahead of the ball and so, too, will your weight. You then allow yourself to move on through, emphasising top half, not legs, to make a good contact.

ADDING HEIGHT TO THE SHORT PITCH

We sometimes see pictures of professional golfers – Seve Ballesteros is a good example – playing a short pitch where there appears to be a lot of hand action. Be realistic about the length of shot being played. The television camera often fails to give a true feeling of the length of shot. Sometimes you are looking at a far longer one than you may imagine. The key here is to realise how the seemingly wristy position at the top of the backswing is created.

The little shot I have previously described, played with a sand iron with plenty of loft – 60 to 62 degrees – will produce plenty of height. The club shaft sits with its full loft at address and through impact and the ball pops up quickly with plenty of stop. The reason why players find it difficult to get height with short pitches is usually that they start with their hands pushed forwards to the left, use wrist action in the backswing which actually de-lofts the club, and then hit the ball with a forward contact rather than brushing the ground beneath it. If you hold your wrists high or forwards at address it will de-loft the club. Conversely, if you can hold your hands low or fractionally back you can add height.

In order to create height, the feeling should be of gripping the club at the end of the shaft and pushing the hands and wrists low at address. This automatically produces quite a wrist angle between the arms and the club shaft. It is this angle we see at the top of the backswing. There is no question of adding wrist action during the swing. In order to open the face, we not only have to turn it out a touch but we also have to push the wrists down. Once again the golden rule is that the club shaft points to your belly button, meaning that the feet have to be wider apart and the legs more bent. The feeling now is of pushing the wrists low and keeping that low wrist action throughout the swing. As this wrist position is taken back in the backswing it automatically produces the appearance of considerable wrist-cock. But the wrist-cock is created at address and not by some movement in the backswing.

From there, the arms and club swing down to the same position through impact as they were at address. The important point is to be able to retain that wrist action right the way through the swing. This means that by the time you get to the follow-through the back of the left hand will be very firm and facing upwards, the left elbow will naturally have drawn away slightly behind you and the face of the club is very much upwards facing, having produced maximum loft through impact.

A common piece of advice is to keep the hands ahead of the ball and never allow the clubhead to take over. There are two dimensions to this. The first is in looking straight at the player across the ball. The advanced golfer is very unlikely to use too much wrist action, seen from this view. The long-handicap player, however, often tries to scoop the ball. The second dimension is the more crucial for the good player. If we look back at the player from the target we should see the hands and clubhead work through correctly without the clubhead passing the hands. It is as though the hands swing along the inside track of a pair of railway lines while the club-head swings out and along the other. The two never cross or meet. In order to achieve this, the feeling is of the hands still being kept very low through impact and the clubhead always working out beyond them. In this way the right wrist stays set back on itself, the left elbow if anything drags away to the left, and the back of the left hand is upwards. In this way a short, high shot can be felt, again with absolutely no wrist action.

The left arm must shorten beyond impact. In this shot, as with most short game shots, the left wrist must stay arched, back of the wrist up, clubface up and out in front. The hands stay low through impact, the clubhead staying out beyond them

Players who play these shots with too much wrist, particularly for shots under 20 yards, soon find they don't work under pressure or from a tight lie. Adopting the correct address position, with any desired wrist action already set, produces the most reliable of shots in a pressure situation.

THE UPHILL PITCH

The danger with a short, uphill pitch is that the ball is left short. One of the easiest ways for the good golfer to drop a shot is to hit the ball just through the green, particularly downwind, to be faced with a short pitch from an uphill lie back again, and to leave the shot 6 or 8 feet short, missing the putt.

Playing the short, uphill pitch is easy; judging the distance can often be difficult. Remember that any uphill shot adds height and takes off distance. With an uphill pitch, abandon your sand iron unless you really do want a shot which is all height and virtually no run at all. The pitching wedge or 9-iron is a much better choice, allowing you to play the shot as though it were a sand iron on a flat lie and to judge the distance correctly.

On the uphill shot, narrow your stance slightly. This ensures that you move forwards rather than being caught hanging back on the right foot. In addition, lean a little bit into the slope, standing vertically, and make sure the swing travels down and up the slope, without stabbing into it. Again, feel that the left arm can shorten away quite naturally and bring the club-head upwards rather than digging in.

The most crucial point with the uphill pitch, however, is to give the ball enough distance and to be determined to get it past the flag.

THE DOWNHILL PITCH

The difficulty with the downhill pitch is entirely the opposite from that of the uphill one. The uphill pitch is easy to play. You are going to make contact with the ground only after the ball is struck. With the downhill shot the

To play the downhill pitch requires a very wide stance, enabling all the weight to be on the left leg throughout, with the right shoulder held high. This immediately gives a steep up and down action without any real wrist action. The clubface can be held open to counteract the downslope, hands at the top of the shaft but wrists low. In the downswing the clubhead must travel **down** the slope, the left leg sinking and bowing out, never rising up. Keep the head still and listen for the ball to land for a sound contact

problem is that the ground potentially gets in the way *before* we ever make contact with the ball. Added to that, the downslope takes off loft, meaning that it is difficult to get height and stop. With the downhill pitch, always choose a sand iron if at all possible. From a severe slope, even with the face open, you won't produce as much loft as you would probably like. But the key is to get a good address position. You have to produce a set up that minimises the chance of the club scuffing the ground before you strike the ball. You need to set yourself to stand out at right angles to the slope, the shoulders following the slope. To do this the stance has to be very wide, a downhill pitch or downhill bunker shot having a much wider stance than any other golf shot. Feel that you let the left knee bend to the left, putting it into a position from where it can bow out to the left as you move through and beyond impact. It is one of the few shots where the left leg bends through impact – never straightening or the whole swing path lifts.

Preferably hold the clubface slightly open, and keep a very high right shoulder at address and the ball fairly well back in the stance. The club shaft should naturally follow the line of the body, never being pushed too far to the left. Have a couple of practice swings, feeling that the club definitely moves *down* the slope beyond impact, allowing the left leg to bend so that the swing can be kept travelling downwards. Rehearse the feeling of bouncing the club on the ground and work at a perfect contact.

If the clubface is held open at address it must be held open through impact to be effective. Ensure, once again, that the club shaft points to your belly button rather than your left shoulder, and take care to keep the ball well towards the toe of the club. It is all too easy, in trying to open the clubface quite dramatically, to nudge the ball towards the socket. If in doubt, look at the ball position relative to the clubhead from directly behind the angle it sits at. In playing the shot, keep the right shoulder just as high as possible at address and through impact, giving steepness to the attack without the need for hand action. Allow the left leg to bow out through impact, moving the club down rather than up, and slide the left arm and elbow away, with left wrist and clubface uppermost.

As with most tricky short shots, any that are ruined are usually the result of looking up too early in your anxiety to see where the ball goes. Concentrate on an up-and-down action, the club feeling to go down the slope after impact, while keeping your eyes firmly on the spot where the ball was. Try to listen for the ball to land rather than being tempted to look up.

LISTENING FOR THE SHORT PITCH

A good feeling with short pitching, particularly from a tightish lie, is to work at listening for the shot rather than looking for it. If you have a couple of practice swings you can *hear* the club bouncing on the ground and in so doing can *feel* the way the club makes contact with the ground and will in turn make contact with the ball.

Under pressure the most common reason for spoiling a short pitch for a low-handicap golfer is simply looking up too soon. The ball is in the air such a short time that it is easy to look up a split second early with anxiety and curiosity. Sometimes it is almost a question of trying to see where you are going at the moment of impact. The feeling with any short pitch over a bunker, particularly from a tight lie, should be to keep your head still and to *listen* for the ball to land. When playing onto a fairly firm green you should certainly hear it.

One of the difficulties in practising with several balls, and keeping your head still, is that you may not know which was the last one hit. This can tempt you to look up early, a bad fault which will then be repeated under pressure.

It is worth developing your own drill to train yourself to stay still without trying to see which ball is which. Aiming to different targets can help. Practising with relatively few balls, making each one count, is sometimes better than hitting too many and allowing bad faults to creep in.

A good exercise is simply to practise short pitching into an umbrella. Use a distance of 8 to 12 yards and keep listening for the ball to hit the umbrella. You can instinctively feel the quality of the contact and will nearly always know where the ball has missed if you don't hear it drop. If you keep your head still on a really short pitch the ball rises out of view. Stay still long enough and it often drops back into the edge of your field of vision.

For the tournament golfer it is essential to be able to play these shots, even from the worst of lies, with the feeling of the eyes being focused on the ground long enough. With a poor lie the head doesn't stay perfectly still but will move to the left to correspond with your taking the divot. It is not exactly a question of 'head still' but more one of keeping the eyes still and learning to use the ears.

LONGER PITCHING

The long pitch from 30 yards to, let's say, 100 yards can be played with the sand iron, pitching wedge or 9-iron. The execution of these shots doesn't usually give problems to lower-handicap golfers, but they are shots which need practising in order to develop accuracy. Most single-figure handicap golfers find these far easier than very short pitches.

Firstly, consider the address position. Remember that gripping up and down the club can vary the distance quite simply. If you go down a pitching wedge a couple of inches it takes off distance without any other change. Look, too, at the ball position. The ball should be played just ahead of centre, allowing you to move into the ball to make good contact. Too far forward and you may mis-hit the odd one; too far back and the contact may become too deep and erratic.

In playing the longer pitch we again want a ball-divot contact. The right shoulder should be held fairly high at address, certainly not with the right elbow and shoulder tucked down. The feeling is one of moving

Tom Watson playing a three-quarter pitch, arms never straying from the body, clubface held up and open through impact and the top half moving through

through the ball with the top half of the body. The head starts opposite the middle of the stance and finishes opposite the left foot. In moving left through impact, the clubhead usually strikes the ball before the swing is quite on target and hence with the clubhead still moving slightly in-to-out in relation to the feet. For most players this tends to produce a push. The line of the feet therefore needs adjusting. We usually describe this as opening the stance but in reality for many people it is simply a question of aiming the feet round to the left until the ball can be started correctly. In turning the feet to the left, it may be necessary to turn the right foot in a touch. If you leave the right foot in its normal position,

square or even turned out, and simply withdraw the left foot, the right foot can often hold you back, restricting movement through the ball. The knees should feel as though they can bend a touch *towards* the target.

The feeling of the swing should be of limiting the length of backswing without any particularly pronounced or early wrist break, but then being able to accelerate through the ball, holding the clubface square beyond impact, back of the left hand firm. The most common problem with pitching is of hitting the ball far too high, by whipping the ball up into the air with excessive hand action. The feeling needs to be of keeping the ball drilled with a penetrating flight, the back of the left hand staying firm, clubface looking on target at the moment of impact and several inches beyond it. The feeling of the divot should be a reasonably shallow one, making sure the clubhead takes the ball and the divot, then comes out again without simply burying the club in the ground.

Players occasionally find that the inside attack produces a tendency to draw the ball rather than push it. These players are probably prone to hooking the full shots. By hitting the ball from the inside with pitches, they start putting drawspin on the ball, the clubface square to the target but closed to the swing path. In this case the remedy is often one of squaring up

With longer pitching and punch shots the real key is to keep a high right shoulder throughout and to let the top half of the body move through towards the target. This gives the necessary ball-divot contact. Ensure that the right foot is never turned out at address but in if anything. This makes the knees feel as though they want to bend a touch towards the target at address, limiting the length of the backswing but allowing good movement through

the stance. Turning the feet left is therefore one of trial and error rather than a totally hard and fast rule.

Let's consider the arm position. The arms hang to the side and stay fairly close to the side. In the throughswing the left arm shouldn't leave the body. It is not a question of pulling the arm in but of the upper body chasing the arm. A club cover held under the left upper arm will give the feeling of body and arm chasing each other. The upper body must be allowed to move through towards the target, putting emphasis on the upper body rather than the legs. The posture in the hips is set at address. This hip angle and posture are maintained throughout the swing, naturally allowing the top half to move through. A useful concept is for the head to start opposite the ball – so slightly ahead of the centre of the stance – and to finish opposite the left instep. This upper body movement corresponds with the divot. The bottom of the swing is saucer shaped. The club moves down into impact, and the body moves a touch left to correspond with taking the divot – the flat part of the saucer base – and then moves on up and through.

DRAWING AND FADING THE PITCH SHOT

The advanced player should be able to put sidespin on a pitch or a punch shot. Putting fade or cutspin on the ball with a wedge is essential, particularly if you want stop on the ball or are playing into a right-left wind. Most good golfers do this relatively easily. It simply means holding the clubface

Joakim Haeggman punching in a wedge with a touch of fade and cut, clubface pulling across the ball through impact and left elbow dragging away behind him

a fraction open at address, possibly going for a less lofted club to counteract this, and then through impact keeping the back of the left hand firm and sliding the clubface fractionally across the ball in an out-to-in direction at the moment of impact. It is as though the path of the swing comes straight into the ball and then simply adds sidespin. In this way added backspin can be achieved by using either of the wedges, or a left to right spin can be felt by using a 9-iron or straighter-faced club.

Many players use this as their standard pitch into the green. In calm conditions it gets good

Bernhard Langer drawing in a pitch, clubface working over through impact and left elbow breaking in

stop. But into a headwind this can sometimes be slightly weak and drop short of where you imagine. The danger point is often where a flag is tucked round behind the right-hand bunker and the cutspin takes off distance.

In order to keep a ball moving forwards, particularly where the flag is on the back of the green or into a left-to-right wind, the feeling should be of being able to draw the ball. Remember that loft kills sidespin. If you set up for an action which would produce a real hook with a 4- or 5-iron, all it will do with a pitching wedge is to keep the ball holding into the cross-wind, giving it more penetration. You can close the clubface quite dramatically with a pitching wedge and it will still be impossible to get a real hook. The feeling can then be of attacking the ball very much from the inside as though trying to wipe the clubface from in-to-out across the ball to produce sidespin. Experimenting with this can help produce a pitch shot which has enough forward power to keep moving to the back of the green and which can hold into a nasty cross-wind on your back. Don't be afraid of experimenting with the shot. You will almost certainly find you can close the clubface much more than you think and attack the shot much more from the inside than you imagine.

JUDGING DISTANCE WITH PITCHING

The usual theory with the pitch, whether short or long, is that you choose the spot on which you want to land the ball and let it run the rest of the way.

Most golfers, pitching from a distance of 15 to 40 or 50 yards, leave the ball short. The shot looks good. As you walk forward you realise the ball is 10 or 15 feet short and instead of one putt you take two. Possibly the real difference between the top 10 players in the world and the rest is that they judge distance around the green just that bit better.

Judging distance can be a real optical illusion. When weighing up the shot it is easy to choose a landing spot which is too short. You imagine you are choosing a spot 5 yards short of the target whereas in reality it is 8 or 10 yards short. You then perhaps pitch the ball short of your landing spot rather than past it. The ball lands 12 yards short rather than 5 yards short, runs 5 yards and there you are, 20 feet short of the flag instead of right by it. Obviously tournament professionals take time and invariably walk forward to look at the shot from the side, choosing their landing spot more accurately. But even if the choice of spot is good, most golfers still constantly come up short. Many golfers attack the flag better, not simply by looking for a landing spot but by thinking far more in terms of the overall length of the shot, whether with pitching, running shots or bunker shots. The distance between the flag and the back of the green is often very illusive. However much a player feels that he can attack the flag, the tendency to leave the ball 6 or 8 feet short instead of 2 or 3 feet past the hole can make the real difference between being a winner and an also-ran.

With a long green and the flag positioned at the back, imagine a pond or bunker right up to the point where you would hope to pitch the ball, and the flag just beyond it. The good golfer is unlikely to hit short in this situation and it promotes boldness.

THE OPEN-FACED CUT SHOT

Learning to open the face of a club correctly is vital for playing good bunker shots. But the open face is also important for certain pitch shots where we want to get extra height.

To open the face of a club we have two approaches. The first is to hold the sand wedge to the ground in front of you with its ordinary maximum loft. The clubface is then turned out to the right to increase the loft. But going hand in hand with this, the club shaft should also be dropped a touch. In this way we have an open clubface sitting out to the right of our target. From here we would instinctively turn the whole clubface and ourselves round to the left, in other words opening the stance.

But as an exercise, and the second approach, take hold of your sand iron again and set it up with its full loft. The club shaft points to your belly button. Now to open the clubface, tip the club back as though the club shaft moves 4 or 5 inches to the right. You have now increased the loft of the club. The top of the club has gone back and also of course moved down an inch or so. To match this, you have to move your belly button back to find the end of the club! This means moving behind the ball, turning your feet round to the left and widening the stance, with well-bent knees, to bring your belly button to find the club! The shaft of the club should still point to you – never to the left shoulder – with club shaft and feet comfortably at right angles to each other.

To see exactly what opening the clubface means, learn to play a short little pitch of 10 yards or so from a nice fluffy lie using a 5- or 6-iron. A blade club is much easier for this experiment than a heel-toe type. Again, take hold of the club in your right hand and lay the club back to increase its loft dramatically. The top of the club goes back and down. You in turn need to move yourself, your feet and your body round, so that once more the club shaft points to your belly button. Again this means widening your stance, lowering your whole stance and getting yourself into a new position. Bend the knees. The leading edge of the club still points at your target but the loft is increased. To play the shot from here – which is of course an exercise which will never be used on the course – the feeling must be of holding the clubface open as you come through impact, keeping the back of the left hand upwards, drawing the left elbow away behind you and feeling that height can be retained. Concentration on the clubface for a few practice swings shows just what can be done.

To learn how to hold the clubface open practise high, tiny pitch shots with a 6-iron. The knees must bend and the wrists work correctly to achieve height. After this a sand wedge seems easy!

The advantage of trying this exercise is that you can develop height only by doing it correctly. It emphasises the feeling of having to hold the clubface open through impact to create loft and backspin. It shows how opening the clubface must go hand in hand with widening the stance, lowering the stance and, indeed, standing far enough away from the ball. The typical wrong action of opening the clubface sees the player turn the toe of the club out but keep the hands to normal height. From there he often simply turns the line of the feet and shoulders to the left but without getting the right relationship of the club shaft still pointing up to him.

Once you can make this feeling then all manner of cut shots become relatively simple, whether using the wedge for height and backspin, fading the ball into a right-to-left wind with a punchy 4- or 5-iron, or feeling the ability to be able to slice the ball round trees if the need arises. For the player with a natural hook or draw it begins to explain how a fade for safety is produced.

THE PUNCH SHOT

Being able to play a long running shot is crucial in approaching the green in windy conditions, with overhanging trees, and also in playing to a two-tier green. With the flag on the top layer of a two-tier green it is usually hopeless to try to pitch the ball on it. The top layer of a two-tier green is very rarely the same size as an ordinary green. The total green is probably still only 28 yards from front to back and the top layer only 13 yards or so deep. Added to this, water tends to drain off the top layer onto the bottom layer and a ball pitched onto the top, even with the best of wedge shots, is often destined to run through. If on the other hand you pitch onto the lower level with a fairly lofted club, the ball stops. The lower level probably gathers moisture and is receptive. So the correct way of tackling this is to play a less lofted club, possibly something like a 7- or 8-iron, which will pitch short and have enough steam to run up onto the top.

In playing these running shots, the action is very much like that of a pitch. The right shoulder must be held high at address and the top half of the body must be allowed to move through impact. Once again we have the feeling of the head starting opposite the middle of the stance and finishing more or less opposite the left foot. There is a movement of, let's say, 3 or 4 inches to the left to correspond with the ball-divot contact. But the club again comes smoothly out of the divot the other side and the clubface must be held squarely on target. In moving onto the ball, the attack is likely to be slightly in-to-out. For many players this again tends to produce a push, which can be counteracted by opening the stance round to the left and turning the right foot in a touch. For other players this slightly in-to-out approach is likely to produce a draw or sometimes almost a hook. For these players the feeling must be of holding the clubface open through impact, and keeping the club looking on target for several inches after the ball is hit.

Remember with these shots that the swing is nearly always longer than you imagine. The feeling must be of cutting the backswing down and accelerating smoothly through impact. The feeling needs to be of a saucer-shaped arc to the swing. We have three possible attacks on the ball. The attack tends to be mirrored in the flight of the shot you produce. If you produce a V-shaped, steep, downward attack, you tend to produce a high, steep shot – ideal for recovery from heavy rough. If you produce a teacup-shaped shot, you will equally produce an inverted teacup shape to your shot. In this case you want a saucer-shaped arc to produce an inverted saucer shape to the shot. The most common problem for the good player is possibly picking up the club too steeply and producing too much wrist action in the takeaway, resulting in a shot with too much height and not enough penetration. Ideally the stance can be fairly wide, allowing movement back slightly onto the right foot and then through onto the left foot, drilling the ball forwards and enabling it to hold its line.

These shots can certainly then be played by imparting some sidespin. The clubface should feel to be held on target through impact, either moving it slightly in-to-out across the back of the ball to produce draw or just pulling it in across the ball at the moment of impact to produce cut. Once the sidespin can be felt with this kind of shot, it can then more easily be developed with longer clubs and full shots.

For the aspiring champion, these are some of the most important shots. A feeling of sidespin combined with the ball finishing on target needs mastering – a little draw, a little fade. This forms the basis for learning a touch of spin with the longer shots and driving.

ALL ABOUT BUNKER SHOTS

THE BASIC BUNKER SHOT

The first key to good bunker shots is to keep the right shoulder high at address and in the throughswing. In this way the top half stays high and moves forward through impact, giving an accurate entry into the sand. Draw one line 2 inches behind the ball and another 4 inches beyond it. Your head starts opposite the line behind the ball, eyes focused on the line. Your head finishes opposite the other line

The simplest way for a medium- and higher-handicap golfer to play bunker shots is to choose a club with plenty of loft and to learn to play the shots with a fairly square clubface. The simplest shot is to have the ball fairly well forward in the stance, set up with a 2-inch gap between the club and the ball, to keep your eyes focused on the sand and to feel that you simply pitch the sand forwards and out onto the green. If the sand comes out, so too does the ball. The stance should be fairly wide, allowing the player to move on through towards the left foot. The right shoulder needs to be held reasonably high at address, certainly not down or with the elbow tucked in, and the feeling must be of allowing the top half of the body to move on through.

The most classic fault in bunker shots is allowing the right shoulder to stay low and allowing the top half to drop behind the ball instead of moving on through. The weight must move through onto the left foot in every bunker shot, but it is not so much a question of leg action as one of the top half moving through. Very often with longer-handicap players, the legs move to the left but the shoulders and head move back to the right. The feeling must always be of the right shoulder staying high and the top half moving through.

For the lower-handicap player, let's assume that the clubface can be held very slightly open. (We will look into this in more detail later.) So, the clubface is turned out a touch, the ball is well forward in the stance, the club shaft points straight up towards

you and there is a 2-inch gap between the club and the ball. Forget about the direction. Simply hold the clubface open, keep your eye on the sand, play the shot and let your head move to the left, with the right shoulder held high. It is the body movement which is crucial to playing the bunker shot well.

Let's explain this further. First of all, draw a line in the sand 2 inches behind the ball and another one 4 inches beyond it. Start with your clubhead, your head and eyes opposite the line behind the ball. By the time you finish the swing the top half of your body will have moved through so that your head and eyes are now opposite the other line. Think of it this way. You set up to the ball with a bend in your hips. As you move on through that bend is retained and the upper body moves towards the flag, right shoulder high. Many players let the legs move to the left but the top half wrongly moves behind the ball. The bend in the hips is undone and turns into the top half arching backwards. The crucial feeling must be that the top half moves through, and this in turn will splash the sand forward.

This, then, is our basic bunker shot. The clubface is held square or slightly open, and the ball is well forward in the stance, with a 2-inch gap between the club and the ball. Stay looking at the sand behind the ball and concentrate on splashing the sand *forward* and out onto the green. If you splash the sand forward the ball pops out with it.

Wrong. If the right elbow and shoulder are held low at address or the right shoulder drops through impact the contact becomes shallow. Here the hips have led, right shoulder dropping

OPENING THE CLUBFACE

Professionals play almost all bunker shots with the clubface open. Most difficulties arise, however, through not understanding how to open the face. As an exercise, sit the club down in the sand with a square face. Now turn it out to the right and lower the shaft of the club. Lowering the shaft must go hand in hand with turning the face out. Now address the ball. Bend the knees and stand far enough away. There are three problems with opening the face.

Firstly, in opening the face the ball tends to get too near the socket. We therefore have to pull it up towards the toe. It must look to be central or towards the toe of the club when viewed from directly behind the clubhead at right angles to the open face. Secondly, the club tends to look awkward. This is particularly so if you have a club with a square leading edge or one where the lie of the club is too upright. If too upright, as you turn the toe out it seems to come off the ground. This is a common reason for lowish-handicap players being prone to shanking bunker shots. Holding the club too far down the grip can have the same effect. The lie of a sand iron is important. Correctly irons, of course, become more upright as we move from 3-iron to pitching wedge. The lie of the sand wedge should never be more upright than the pitching wedge, but preferably slightly flatter. In most sand-wedge shots we sink through impact and never brace the left

Frank Nobilo playing a 'semi-splash', clubface well open, hands at the top of the club, wrists low and standing well away from the ball. The clubface is held open through impact and the club **bounced** on through to a fairly restricted finish, clubface looking upwards and splashing the sand forwards

leg. Personally I like my sand wedge to have the same lie as my 7-iron, making it easy to open the clubface with a low wrist position.

Thirdly, opening the clubface often feels awkward. The grip on a club is not completely round but slightly egg-shaped, with the pointed bit of the egg at the back of the grip. To open the clubface you must first turn it out and then grip it. The pointed part of the egg-shaped grip will now come in a different part of your hands.

So the key factors are to open the clubface by lowering the wrists, to keep the ball towards the toe of the club and to overcome any awkward feelings with the hands.

From here we have to learn to hold the clubface open through impact. Many golfers starting with a square clubface find it reasonably easy to come through with a square clubface. Opening the face at address tends to make them use even more wrist action than normal, often closing the clubface at the moment of impact. The feeling must be of continuing to hold the face open. As an exercise, put the club down into the sand and scoop some sand onto the clubface. Then simply take the club through towards your follow-through position, holding the sand on the face of the club. Toss the sand upwards in front of you. In doing this the back of the left hand must stay up, wrist a touch arched, never collapsed, and the left elbow must if anything slide away behind you. This keeps the face looking up

At the finish of the greenside splash shot the left elbow breaks away, the clubface pulling across the ball to add cutspin and then staying in a face up position in the finish, left wrist firm

rather than working into a toe-up position. Do you throw the sand up in front of you or do you close the face and throw the sand round behind you? Again, scoop the sand on to the clubface, hold it there, keep the back of left hand looking upwards, let the left elbow slide behind you and feel the sand being tossed up and out. The feeling in playing the shot must be the same.

Visualise the clubface being held in a face-up position as it cuts beneath the ball, and then continue in this sort of position as you move on through. Crucial to holding the face open is to make friends with the bottom of the club. The club now has a bouncing bottom rather than a cutting leading edge. The feeling should be of bouncing the club in the sand, awareness of the flange often enabling players to feel the clubface held open more easily.

A key to this movement is the way in which the left arm works. Remember that in every shot we play the left arm has to shorten and fit into

One of the best disciplines for learning to open the clubface in a bunker is to tackle the short with a 6- or 7-iron. The clubface is laid back, ball near enough the toe of the club (not the socket), club shaft pointing to the belly button, the knees have to be well bent, and the whole stance turned and aimed left to pop the ball on target. The clubface has to be held open through impact, back of the left hand upwards

a fairly small space. The arm must not fold away inwards as it does in the long game. Players with active hand action in the long game, possibly with draw or hook, often tend to use too much hand action in the bunker shot. The clubface if anything closes.

The correct action of the left arm is to make sure the back of the left hand stays up, feeling the left arm break outwards and slide behind you as the swing continues. For the very gifted golfer all he needs to feel is the clubface, and the left arm will move in response to it. But frequently the player who hooks needs to create a definite feeling with the left hand and left arm to get the right action.

Trying to play bunker shots with a 6- or 7-iron, laying it back and opening it up like a sand wedge, will demonstrate just how the clubface has to be held open and kept open through impact, stance widening, knees bending.

DIRECTION IN A BUNKER

The usual advice in playing bunker shots is that you open the clubface, open the stance and swing out-to-in. It is advice which is usually misunderstood and misinterpreted.

If the clubface is held open, with the stance square, you instinctively know the ball will pop away to the right. In learning to play good bunker shots don't worry initially about the direction of the shot. Aim at the target, open the clubface slightly and allow the ball to pop 6 feet or so away to the

With an open clubface the ball will pop away to the right. The whole stance has to be turned away to the left. The club **may** come back on the outside of the ball target line but it comes back on the inside of the line of the stance. The cut is added by pulling the clubface in across the ball and holding the clubface open through impact

right. Once you feel comfortable with this, turn the whole stance and swing round to the left. Remember the golden rule that the club shaft is going to point to your belly button. In order to get your stance in the right position you need to move the whole stance round in a circle to the left so that the shaft of the club still points directly towards you. Very often the advice to open the stance simply means that players withdraw the left foot and put the right foot forward. The line of the stance is open but the player is all at odds with himself. The feeling must be of the leading edge of the club going more or less on target, perhaps a touch to the right, with the line of the stance away to the left and the club shaft still pointing directly to you. Check that these angles are correct.

With the right shoulder held high and the wrists held low at address the swing can be steep. The stance is opened round to the left, club shaft still pointing to the belly button. The swing may feel to come back high and out-to-in. In reality it is always well inside the line of the feet, but across the line of the shot

As far as swinging out-to-in is concerned, we have to understand exactly what is meant. There are two meanings of 'out-to-in'. Are we looking at a swing which is out-to-in in relation to the line from the ball to the target, or are we looking at a swing which is out-to-in in relation to the line of the feet and shoulders? If you look at professional golfers you will see that the swing is nothing like as out-to-in as most people imagine, except in very exceptional circumstances. It may in fact be very slightly out-to-in in relation to the ball to target line but is certainly not out-to-in in relation to the line of the feet. If you stand behind a tournament professional playing a bunker shot and imagine these two lines, you will actually see that the club is taken back very much *inside* the line of the feet but possibly almost directly back on the line of the shot. The club then comes down more or less on the line of the shot. The key to getting sidespin is that the clubhead then cuts away behind the player at the moment of impact. The clubface is held open and sidespin is very simply imparted.

Amateur golfers often have the feeling of trying to swing very out-to-in, awkwardly cutting across themselves and hitting the ball from the neck of the club. Most golfers get into difficulties by being far too out-to-in rather than taking the club away too much on the inside. Remember that if you get a good address position with the ball well forward, club shaft pointing towards you, it is simply a question of aiming the feet left and allowing for the ball to pop away to the right as you add a bit of sidespin through impact. The right shoulder must be kept high at address and providing this is done, the direction of the swing is unlikely to cause any real problems. Players who take the club away too shallow and on the inside usually do so because the right shoulder is held low and the right elbow tucked in at address. Get a good address position, forget about swinging out-to-in and simply concentrate on the open face through impact and imparting back- and sidespin.

THE SEMI-SPLASH SHOT AND SPLASH SHOT

There are two ways of playing the splash shot. I like to describe them as the semi-splash and full splash.

When you play on an inland course the sand may look soft and fluffy but very often there is a hard layer just an inch or so beneath the surface. The correct shot from these bunkers is to play a semi-splash shot. In this the wrist action is reasonably firm and the swing fairly restricted. It is simply a question of holding the clubface slightly open, using a reasonably wide stance, keeping the club open through impact and allowing the top half of the body to move on through. The swing path is wide and shallow with no pronounced pick-up in the backswing. The hands remain fairly firm through impact and if the sole of the club should make contact with the hard part beneath the sand, the problem is fairly minimal. At the end of the swing the top half moves through towards the target, right shoulder high, and the club finishes at roughly shoulder height.

The face can be held well open and the shot will produce plenty of height and stop. It will certainly get out of anything you can see out of!

The other shot, the full splash, is more appropriate at a seaside course where there is a continuous depth of sand and never any feeling of hitting a hard patch beneath. In the full splash shot there is a feeling of plenty of hand action. The feeling once more is of opening the clubface but the swing is now full and very, very slow. It is a shot for the advanced golfer. The feeling at impact is literally of the right hand throwing the clubface underneath the ball and almost as though scooping or tossing the ball up and out. It is exactly the opposite of the feeling the medium- and high-handicap player should have. The right hand literally does move the clubhead beneath the ball and toss it forward and out and up. The finish of the swing should now see the club shaft landing on the left shoulder; the hands will have loosened their grip on the club and the wrists will be fully cocked back.

The thought for this shot is to imagine that you are 90 years old – your swing will therefore lack much speed and oomph – and you swing the club all the way back and all the way through as slowly as you possibly can. If you say to yourself, 'All the way back and all the way through' and make the swing last the length of time it takes to say that, you won't go far wrong!

This shot is possible only when the lie really is perfect, when you know there is a good cushion of sand beneath the ball and when you want to get plenty of height. The swing is now a very steep U shape rather than the wider swing of the semi-splash. It is particularly useful when you need to get the ball up very quickly, situations like the road hole bunker at St Andrews and where elevation from a good lie is the key requirement.

The good player needs to be able to play all three shots – the standard one with the square face for recovery from poor lies, the semi-splash for the inland course and the full splash from soft, powdery sand or when plenty of height is required.

Miguel Angel Jimenez playing a full splash shot from a deep seaside bunker. Here the swing is full and slow, taking the club all the way through into a full, lazy finish. The right hand literally tosses the ball up and out for real height – only possible with plenty of soft sand

Greg Norman throwing the ball up and out with the right hand for a full, high splash shot

VARYING DISTANCE IN THE BUNKER

To work at different distances for greenside bunker shots, look for a particular distance as your starting point. A bunker shot of 12 yards will give you a good, standard short-distance shot – long enough to get out of most greenside bunkers but short enough not to run through the other side. Learn this as your standard and you then have a distance from which to move up and down.

The next distance to work at is 8 yards. This can be so short as to be intimidating, particularly from a totally flat bunker with no lip. To play this shot, try a combination of holding the club a little more firmly and simply shortening the swing, using a semi-splash shot with a slightly open clubface. Feel that the swing is kept under control and kept short, but do remember that you must still accelerate smoothly through the ball to get sand and ball out reliably. The danger is of taking too long a backswing and decelerating, or alternatively of being too ambitious and trying to play a shot that is just too short for comfort. There must still be a certain degree of acceleration to get through the sand. Pace off a distance of 8 yards, put down a tee peg to practise to and get the feeling of this as a very separate shot.

The next distance to look at is one of 20 yards. This distance can be one of the most daunting, particularly with a long bunker to negotiate and little room for landing on the green. One way of playing it is to play a semi-splash shot with a square clubface, just concentrating on a bit more speed and possibly going into the sand slightly closer to the ball. Perhaps the most straightforward way of playing the 20-yard bunker shot is to play a full splash shot but with the clubface perfectly square and concentrating on the sand an inch behind the ball. In this way the feeling of the swing is full but very slow, the square clubface giving the added distance. The 30-yard shot can be tackled in much the same way – a full splash shot with a square face, a touch more speed, and still taking some sand.

Beyond that distance, the easiest way of approaching the shots is to play with a pitching type of action, thinking of a ball-divot type of contact, striking the ball and then the sand without risking any sand first.

Be specific about the distances you are playing. See each shot as a very definite, separate skill and don't get caught by indecision about your approach to the shot.

DOWNHILL BUNKER SHOTS

The downhill bunker shot is one of the most difficult of all. The downslope takes off loft and does literally get in the way of making a good contact. The downslope need not be steep to cause difficulties.

At address make sure your shoulders follow the slope of the ground, your body out at right angles to the slope. The stance for a downhill bunker shot needs to be wide – probably the widest of any shot we play. The feeling is of sitting out on the left leg, with the absolute minimum of weight

steadied on the right. The right shoulder needs to be held very high, the clubface kept open to the ball. Keeping the right shoulder high encourages a steep up-and-down action without having to use excessive wrist action. The feeling must then be of looking at the sand behind the ball and following through down the slope.

The real difficulty with a downhill bunker shot is to get height and stop. For the medium-handicap golfer the priority is to get out.

For the advanced golfer the feeling with a downhill bunker shot should be like that of the full splash shot. It should be one of holding the clubface open and allowing the right hand to toss the clubface under the ball and to throw the ball out with right hand action. This should then see the hands loosen on the club just beyond impact and the club shaft land on the left shoulder. It really is a question of tossing the ball up, with the right hand almost scooping it out, left wrist being allowed to flop back on itself. The weight must sink onto the left leg as you move through impact, again with

The downhill bunker shot requires the widest stance of any golf shot, all the weight on the left foot, right shoulder as high as possible. The clubface can be held open, the club picked up in the backswing from right shoulder and arm, and, for the top class golfer, the right hand then allowed to pass the left and actually **throw** the sand and ball up and out. By the end of the swing the hands will have had to loosen on the club, right wrist flopping the club through onto the left shoulder

Standing above the ball, bending the knees, wrists low and holding the clubface up and open through impact into a restricted finish

emphasis on a high right shoulder. In this way you should be able to produce height combined with a ball that stops reasonably softly.

UPHILL BUNKER SHOTS

Mark James playing a short uphill bunker shot with a pitching action, letting the top half move through and forwards

Normally an uphill shot is relatively easy. We make contact with the slope only after the ball has gone. This is exactly the *problem* with the uphill bunker shot. In a short splash shot from a greenside bunker we want to take sand behind the ball. With an uphill lie this can become difficult, for there is *no sand* directly behind the ball, just air.

If you make the mistake of standing in a perfectly upright position, the danger is of hitting the ball cleanly, without cushioning the blow, instead of producing a proper splash shot. The ball can easily go too far. So from a gentle uphill lie, in a relatively flat but sloping bunker, the feeling should now be of hanging slightly back on the right foot so that the shoulders again follow the slope. The feeling is one of trying to produce a splash shot, still going into the sand slightly behind the ball and out beyond. Loft should be no problem so that the clubface is held only slightly open, just sufficient to bounce with the flange, not dig with the leading edge. The feeling should be of looking at the sand behind the ball and splashing it out, but still putting plenty of emphasis on letting the top half and weight move through onto the left foot and up the slope. Think of the sand you are trying to take – enough before the ball and not too much beyond it.

One of the difficult greenside bunker shots – a splash shot from an uphill lie. Here there is no sand behind and level with the ball and the danger is a clean contact. Hang back to let the shoulders follow the slope and still focus the eyes on the sand behind the ball. Splash through the sand and out the other side, concentrating on taking enough sand before the ball and not too much after it

On a sharp uphill lie, from virtually beneath the face of the bunker, remember that the upslope acts as a launch pad. The steeper the upslope the easier it is to get elevation. So from a very steep uphill lie there is no difficulty in getting height; the problem is often in making the ball go far enough. The feeling is simply of standing upright, head opposite the ball and looking half an inch below it, hitting firmly into the bank and the ball popping up.

This shot is all about getting a good address position. Try to find the correct position for the *right* foot, getting far enough away from the ball. Then hoist yourself up from the right foot to stand in a vertical position directly opposite the ball. If you feel slightly out of position, make the best of it rather than shuffling around and losing balance. Grip down the club if, as easily happens, you find yourself too close to the ball. Look at the sand just below the ball and beat into it. From a steep lie it can't go far, so be bold. Remember that, as with most uphill lies, the tendency is for the ball to go left rather than right.

POOR LIES AND EXPECTATIONS

A plugged ball should never cause problems for a good golfer. Hold the clubface square, look just behind the ball and beat it forwards and out. The problem is trying to get backspin. Even if the clubface is opened, the ball is likely to run on landing. But the shot is easy to execute.

Difficulties can arise where the ball lies in a footprint. A deep footprint should be tackled in exactly the same way; just aim at getting the ball out on the green and allow for plenty of run. The clubface can again be held square. The more difficult shot is from a shallow footprint. From a deep one we know the ball can't travel far; from a shallow one there is a danger of the ball flying out with too much speed. In this case the swing needs to be limited for speed and length, holding the clubface square or slightly open if the lie allows, and taking care, of course, not to scrape any sand on the backswing. The wrists are held firm, holding the clubface square or open through impact and again allowing the top half to move through with the right shoulder held high.

With a fairway bunker shot the lie determines the shot to be played. If the lie is perfect and the whole ball sits above the sand, the aim should be of taking it as cleanly as possible. Don't shuffle in the feet or you risk digging in too deep. Stand on top of the sand, look at the back or even towards the top of the ball and concentrate on a perfectly clean strike. If the contact is pure, expect the ball to go up to a club length further than normal, like a flier from light rough. Expect backspin on landing to be reduced. There is no reason why a long iron or wood shouldn't be used, providing the footing can be firm and balance maintained. The main consideration must always be the club needed to negotiate any lip to the front of the bunker. Many a professional falls foul of choosing too ambitious a club and failing to make sufficient height.

If the ball sits even fractionally below the surface of the sand it becomes impossible to strike completely cleanly. Now the contact must be more like a ball-divot strike, taking no sand behind the ball but a little beyond. The most crucial factor is the strike, all the concentration going on this to produce the anticipated length to the shot. If the tiniest quantity of sand gets between clubface and ball, distance can be lost quite dramatically.

With a long fairway bunker shot strike the ball cleanly if it sits perfectly, with the equivalent of a divot if it sits down at all. For a clean contact look slightly higher on the ball than normal and anticipate a flier where it might go 10 yards further than the same shot from grass

10 THINK YOUR WAY TO BETTER GOLF

Winners on the pro circuit don't always have perfect swings. In fact, they don't often have perfect swings. To win requires a strong mental approach. Self-belief and confidence, combined with a consistent method, go a long way towards success. Here, then, are some of the keys to winning.

CHOOSING AND NOMINATING A TARGET

It is vital in every shot we play to choose a target. Most players imagine that they do this, but very few really do. It is easy to look down the fairway, think that you don't want to go into the bunker on the right or the rough on the left and simply look at some general space down the middle of the fairway. In reality, your target should be absolutely pinpointed. It is not a question of making a vague choice; the target must be specific. For this reason it is sometimes much easier to hit the ball straight on a narrow, tree-lined course than a seemingly wide-open one. The latter can lure you into choosing approximate targets, while the tight course tends to pinpoint your attention to specific ones. Ideally you should also choose a target at the right distance. It is preferable to choose a specific landing spot on the fairway rather than some distant church spire on the horizon.

An excellent discipline is to practise hitting balls on the practice ground into an open umbrella. This gives a very clear visual picture, focusing your attention and pinpointing your shots. You can then take the same 'picture' out on the golf course and imagine the open umbrella sitting there to collect every ball you hit.

The choice of a target is particularly important with a punishing hazard on one side of the fairway. Club golfers always aim too close to the obstacle. If they want to miss it they will try to miss it by 2 yards. The professional golfer will usually try to

Laura Davies in action. We all want to hit the ball further but be realistic. Don't try to put on 20 yards of length in one go. The swing becomes erratic. Set yourself realistic targets on the way to being Number One

miss it by 22 yards! It must never be a question of looking at the hazard and thinking of going left of it. The choice of a specific target is crucial, aiming the clubface there, directing the stance and concentrating on positioning.

Aiming away from the flag can cause problems. The flag seems to act as a magnet and if positioned just over a bunker will often draw the player to aim too ambitiously. Once again, the target must be definite. It is not just a case of aiming vaguely left or right of the flag but rather of seeing in your mind's eye some specific target on the green – perhaps the colourful umbrella you practise to – and focusing your attention on that.

A marvellous exercise is to nominate the target you are aiming for on every shot. This focuses your attention, prevents wishy-washy choices and lets you be realistic about your own accuracy. How often do we hit a shot that finishes up well and receives praise but in reality we know it wasn't entirely what we meant or where we had chosen! We usually accept the praise graciously without admitting the error. By nominating the target out loud to a partner or caddie, it gives a sterner test and a more realistic appraisal of our own game.

RECOVERY SHOTS AND RISK TAKING

It is a sad fact that the longer the handicap of the player, the more ambitious he or she is likely to be with recovery shots. Long-handicap players hate to zigzag. If they want to miss an obstacle they try to avoid it by a yard or so and often hate the idea of trying to weave a crooked path to the hole. The long-handicap golfer often wants to hit straight through trees, rain shelters, brick walls – anything but aim away to the side.

The key to good recovery shots is to consider just what you stand to gain or lose. It is so easy to be in a situation in the rough where you look at the shot and imagine you can get the ball on the green. Yes, perhaps you can, once in 20 times. But the point to consider is what you stand to lose if the shot is not the one in 20. Are you really going to achieve anything by taking the risk? Very often we attempt shots to the green where in reality the hopes of getting the length are very remote. If it is going to take two shots to get to the green, why not allow it to be two easy ones rather than trying unrealistically to make it one?

Particularly around the green, players are often overly ambitious. The key question to ask yourself is, 'Am I in a two-shot situation or a three-shot situation?' Ask yourself how many times out of ten you would expect to get down in two. Very often your expectation is only two or three out of ten and yet you cannot resist playing the more difficult shot instead of the easier one. Sometimes a risky little pitch over a bunker actually achieves very little. You may land the ball where you meant to but have very little chance of pulling it up close. A far simpler shot played to the side can leave you just as much chance of getting down in one putt without the risks involved. Some people are gamblers at heart and other people are not.

Shots which cause particular problems to good golfers are the par 5s where we feel we should get on in two. Very often there is some bunker or other obstacle 50 or 60 yards in front of the green waiting to trap us. From that bunker it may be impossible to get onto the green. The player who flirts with danger in trying to reach the green with the second shot often comes unstuck. Instead of making a fairly easy five, he finishes with a six or seven. Sometimes a risky shot onto the green may leave an impossible putt or have very little chance of actually holding the green. A shot played to the front apron, with far less risk, gives just as much chance of making a four.

Professional golfers often take more time and care over their recovery shots than any others. The key is to think precisely where you want to finish before you hit the shot. Get back to safety at all costs

Good old-fashioned cross bunkers often spell disaster. If the bunker is just in front of the green then little may be lost if you go in it. The difference in playing a little pitch over it or a bunker shot is minimal. But it is tempting to take on cross bunkers simply because they are there. You may try for a risky carry but can't make the green anyway. Here the danger is that if bunkered you can't find the green with the next one. Obviously it is impossible to say when one should go for a shot and when not. Some people enjoy playing their game like Seve Ballesteros or Arnold Palmer. Others find a Bernhard Langer or Nick Faldo approach more to their liking.

But remember that for every situation on the golf course there is a correct way of playing the shot. Common sense sits right there on your left shoulder, and you should listen to it; it doesn't need to know whether you are one under par or 12 over par, winning your match or losing it. Play the shot regardless of how you are scoring. Don't become over-ambitious because you are doing well, or in an attempt to make up for past errors. Don't suddenly become cautious because you think you are winning.

Think things out rationally, even under the greatest of pressure, decide on a reasonable expectation, and if in doubt ask yourself what Bernhard Langer would do and try to do the same!

BAD WEATHER BLUES

In a medal competition one group of players can play their round in beautiful sunshine and another in a howling wet gale. But remember that bad weather also affects everyone else on the golf course. In matchplay, if it is raining on you it is also raining on your opponent.

Bad weather should be seen as a specific challenge. In a strokeplay competition bad weather usually wipes out the bottom 60 per cent of the field. They simply can't cope with atrocious conditions. Anyone with a less than perfectly balanced swing is likely to be blown inside out. Those who are not mentally tough start worrying about their scores and blaming the conditions instead of relishing the challenge. The best players in a competition will often love the idea of bad weather for this very reason – it produces a smaller number of potential winners.

The key to playing in bad weather is to remain cheerful, have a nice bright umbrella which says something about your attitude and keep your equipment dry and your feelings positive. The more you smile and look as though you are enjoying yourself, the more frustrating for your fellow competitors. The key to a good swing is to maintain perfect balance and timing. When the wind blows, balance deteriorates. If you have worked at a swing where you can hold your balance until the ball lands, there is room for a little deterioration without harmful side-effects. If your swing is untidy anyway, this is when errors show. When playing in a high wind try to hold the finish of your swing, preferably with the arms and club right through but certainly with the legs totally balanced, for a good count of 5 or 6. It is difficult to do but it keeps you making your best swing just as often as possible.

In a matchplay situation it is largely a question of attitude. If you give the impression to your opponent that you are thoroughly enjoying and relish the challenge, then you will be a hard man to beat.

For the aspiring champion it is certainly worth playing golf from time to time in appalling conditions. If you have scheduled a game or a practice session, go out and test yourself. Learn to play well in poor weather. You have to face it in tournaments.

KNOWING YOUR DISTANCES

In playing any shot we tend to see the directional errors earlier than we see the distance ones. If you hit an 8-iron to the green and the shot is 10 yards right or left of the flag, the impression is of a very poor shot. By contrast, you can hit the ball straight at the flag and be 15 yards short. The shot looks extremely good – until you walk onto the green and see where it really is.

We tend to be more concerned with direction because we see the error before we see the distance error; it is more obvious. How often one walks to the green imagining the three-foot putt for a birdie only to find it expand to 6 or 7 yards as you get close. Directional error is clear to see; the distance error becomes apparent far later.

It is essential to know how far you hit the ball with each iron. It is also vital to know your distances on the course accurately. The advent of yardage charts on many courses does the work for us, but many golfers are still unrealistic about the length they pitch the ball. Work with the yardage chart on your own course. If there isn't one available, measure your own distances and use these religiously. Many players use a yardage chart away from home but by failing to use it at home have insufficient real knowledge of the true distance they hit.

Once you know how far you hit the ball through the air, with, let's say, a 5-iron, you should find a 10-yard gap between adjacent clubs. Usually this reduces to 7 or 8 yards between the 3-iron and 2-iron and may increase between a 9-iron and pitching wedge; but basically you hope for a 10-yard gap.

When playing into the wind, mentally add on distance. Professionals will talk in terms of a 1-, 2-, 3- or 4-club wind or alternatively a 10-, 20-, 30- or 40-yard wind. Be prepared to add on the distances and to trust the yardage.

Players often think they can judge distances accurately with the eye. And yet, put 10 low-handicap players in an unfamiliar situation on the golf course, ask them the distance to the flag and the guesses can be between 120 and 180 yards for the same shot! We simply do not judge distances as accurately as we think. Just as we wear a watch to tell the time, or use a speedometer in our car, so the use of pacing or yardage charts to work out distances can only enhance a player's knowledge of the golf course.

On your own course you get to know the clubbing from certain points. On unfamiliar courses, particularly courses overseas, the more accurate your knowledge of the golf course the greater the security you have in choosing the right club.

An excellent discipline is to play 18 holes giving yourself a point every time your shot to the green from more than, say, 50 yards finishes on the green past the flag. Top-class tournament professionals find this scoring zone far more often than even good amateurs. It has great advantages. Firstly, it allows for a 90 per cent shot still to make the green. Secondly, it well avoids the bunkers short of the putting surface. Thirdly, it allows for the more common tendency to underclub rather than overclub.

If as an exercise you plot on a grid the position relative to the flag of your 18 shots to the green, these should by rights be centred round the hole. For most people the tendency to underclub means that the spots would normally be centred round a point well short of the flag and often noticeably to one side or the other.

Find this scoring zone on the green past the flag more often and this is frequently the simplest route to better scoring. Good golf is far more a question of hitting the ball the right length when within reach of the green, or just around it, than one of hitting the ball straight.

THE WORLD IS ROUND

Professional golfers – and being one, I can say this – are not always renowned for their intelligence. But one thing we do know, which seems to escape the knowledge of many amateur golfers, is that the world is round! Many amateurs still apparently believe it to be flat.

Let me explain what I mean. The amateur golfer often plays all his golf as though playing on a flat earth, seeming to imagine that the end of the world lies just beyond the back of the green. He often has a totally irrational fear of the ball travelling through the back of the green – perhaps worrying that it will fall away into outer space or into the clutches of man-eating tigers or bogeymen!

In reality, of course, although the world is round it looks flat. Judging distance into a green is often hampered by optical illusions. When approaching a green the distance from front to back is often foreshortened. Most greens are at least 24 yards long and the average probably around 28 to 30 yards. But this distance from front to back can seem to squash up into nothing. If the pin is at all behind centre on the green it usually looks much closer to the back than it really is. We then perhaps have a bank and a slope away behind the green with some sort of obstacle, perhaps bushes or out of bounds, beyond this. The distance from the flag to the back of the green seems squashed up, the distance from the back of the green to the top of the bank is foreshortened and the distance from there to the eventual trouble appears to disappear into nothing. It is very easy to approach a green imag-

When you look at a green from the fairway it often looks shallow from front to back, giving the illusion of very little space beyond the flag. This promotes under clubbing. From the side the true length of the green and the club players' tendency to underclub is very obvious

ining that the flag is 3 or 4 yards from the back of the green, that the slope away starts another yard or two from there and that the bushes or out of bounds are only another 4 or 5 yards further. In reality, if you pace off the distance there is much more room than meets the eye. Instead of it being 6 or 7 yards from the flag to the bushes it is probably 20 yards or more.

But our flat-earth golfers, who never appreciate the distance beyond the flag, are always afraid of what might happen, and they constantly underclub. Given the choice between two clubs, a 5-iron or a 6-iron, the amateur golfer will nearly always choose the 6. Partly it is his fear of what happens if he passes the flag, and partly he probably has a friendlier disposition in the first place towards his 6 than his 5. Give a professional golfer the same choice and he will nearly always opt for the 5-iron.

When you watch other people play to a flag while standing to the side of the green, it always seems absurd that they never hit the ball right up to the flag. By definition, of course, we are short of the flag when we tee off. Many golfers then stay short of the flag all the time until the ball goes into the hole, never passing it whether on the shot to the green, the approach shot or the long putt.

A key to playing attacking golf is to know the distance between the flag and the trouble. If you know you have 20 yards to play with, you can confidently take an extra club. If you are unrealistic about the distance your attempts at clubbing are likely to be on the cautious side; very rarely will you pass the flag.

KEEP FIRMLY IN THE PRESENT

Think only of the shot facing you *now*. Playing good golf requires that you stand on the first tee and hit the shot to the best of your ability, then the next and so on. At the end of 18 holes add the score. Hit it, forget it, walk. One boring old shot after another until the round is completed.

The danger is of looking back and looking forward. Looking back goes something like, 'I wish I hadn't had an 8 on the first.' You play the second hole depressed at thoughts of the first. You feel lower and lower, hole after hole looking backwards to the initial disaster. The only thing that wipes out the memory of the 8 on the first is when you take 10 on the ninth! Or perhaps you stand on a tee hoping you don't hook out of bounds like you did the day before, or maybe even at the same tournament last year. Just how far back do some golfers think?

Then, at the ninth, most club golfers (and some pros) can't resist adding the score and mentally doubling it. The club golfer is usually working out his potential new handicap before the tenth hole is completed. In the 1992 Canadian Open, Fred Couples played the first nine of the last round in 30. Yippee! A 60 on the cards. No; he came home in 47.

But looking back may also arise for the professional when that well-meaning lady responsible for sending your scores back to the scorecard, pops out from behind a bush by the sixth green. 'Hello, can I have your scores for the fourth, fifth and sixth.' Having tried to cast them from your mind, you rack your brain. 'Scores for Saunders 4, 7, 4.'

'Oh,' she says. 'You're the first one to take 7 on that hole. How did it happen?' With mumblings of having holed a splendid 10-foot putt to save it being an 8, you trundle off to the seventh tee. Halfway up your backswing you hear her 'whispering' over the walkie talkie. 'Can you imagine a professional taking 7 on a silly little hole like that.' Need I say more?

Looking forwards is equally destructive. For club golfers it is usually thoughts of the prize. Halfway up the sixteenth you start thinking, 'Now if I could just make a birdie up here, par on 17 and a birdie on 18 I could break 70. Wouldn't that be grand.' Your thoughts start racing ahead. Thoughts of the money for pros; thoughts of the prizes for amateurs. 'Perhaps it'll be more cut glass, or a Filofax. I really am an unlucky golfer. I never seem to win anything I really want.' With thoughts of all those other prizes running through your head, the birdie probably doesn't happen. The seventeenth is probably played with more concern over the prizes, the handicap and so on. Another shot dropped. And then – horrors – you play the eighteenth thinking of the speech, quite sure you have won but perhaps wishing you could be second and avoid the dreaded public thank-yous. Instead of calmly walking the eighteenth fairway you find yourself rehearsing the speech, your mind totally ignoring the task in hand. Pros do it too. Have you noticed Nick Faldo and Mark James always muttering to themselves as they walk? It's the speech being rehearsed!

At the end of the day mental strength and positive thinking is the key to winning

So the first key is to live firmly in the present. As soon as you look forward and think 'What if ...?', this equals *stress*. You put unnecessary pressure on yourself. The same rule follows for matchplay. Never mind if you were 5 up and are now only 2 up; live for the moment. Keep the future and the past firmly out of your thoughts. Play one shot at a time.

THE ART OF MATCHPLAY

Matchplay is very different from strokeplay. Now you have an opponent to centend with. Some say you should pit your wits against your adversary; others that you should play the course. The latter is usually wiser; the former what inadvertently happens.

The first aim should be to play the course. If you go round in a lower score than your opponent you will invariably win. If not, he wins. But it is all too easy to be influenced by your opponent's play. You stand on the tee and watch your opponent carve the ball out of bounds. The first mistake is that you think to yourself, 'Oooh, good.' The second mistake is that you hadn't taken your driver from the bag in readiness. So, instead of the driver you arm yourself with a 3-wood but hit it straight down the middle. 'Got you,' you think. But maybe you haven't. Your opponent crashes his 3-off-the-tee in anger down the fairway. But you think nothing of it. And then for the second shot, instead of your 3-wood you go for safety with a beautifully controlled 5-wood. 'I *have* got you,' you think. But maybe you haven't. Your opponent launches himself into another driver, lands it on the green 10 inches from the hole and there you are still 60 yards short, feeling hard done by. A demoralised pitch and three putts later the hole is his not yours. He is puffed up with confidence, 'Well, there's a turn up for the books,' he mutters, making matters worse by recounting the tale to his friend playing behind as they pass on the next fairway. You feel robbed of a hole you fool-ishly thought was in the bag. But in medal play, you would have played your own game and been oblivious of his.

The second rule with matchplay is that big swings can take place. You can be 5 up and lose; equally you can be 5 down and win – if you just keep going. The golden rule when in the lead is never to feel even just the tini-est bit of sympathy for your opponent. If 5 up don't fall for the comment of 'I am sorry I'm not giving you a game' – particularly if your opponent looks alarmingly young, very old, tearful or is in receipt of umpteen strokes. The golf course and your own inadequacies are giving you the game! But how easy it is to fall for that one. Standing at 5 up after the tenth, you decide to try a 2-iron on the next tee, dropping it to the ground to make the strike more testing than from a peg. Back to 4 up! Then, silly idiot, not wanting to be beaten by the 2-iron (which now seems far more important to conquer than your opponent) you try it again on the next tee. 3 up. Then, giving a stroke, you lose the next and back to 2. 'My wife always says that 2 up and 5 to play never wins,' he chuckles. 'Have you heard that one?' 'Yes,' you think, 'and I bet she's a treasure to play against, too!'

A hole in one from your opponent sees him win the next. His excite-ment and your frustration at the next and the game is back to all square. 'Oh, I feel so much better now,' he says and you kick yourself all the way home to defeat for that misguided sympathy!

The last real rule of matchplay is that you must never, ever wish your opponent ill! When he is playing from the bunker don't think 'I hope he thins it into the gorse bush.' If he does the feeling of guilt will do you no good! But if instead he pops it out 3 feet from the hole you are likely to be demoralised. Whenever he stands over the ball imagine it will be a perfect shot, whether a long putt, a bunker shot or the hardest drive on the course. If it is you are ready for it. If not – and very few are – you are lifted by his errors, not deflated by his successes. In this way you are far more likely to learn to play the course, ignore your opponent and learn the real skill of matchplay.

KEEP A CONSTANT EFFORT

See the game as being made up of a number of separate shots. Just play each to the best of your ability. Don't aim for making a score but just let it happen. A real key is to assess your motivation for shots. Champions want to do their best shot every time; club golfers often have a fluctuating level of effort. One shot seems very important – perhaps they are being watched; maybe it is a shot over water – perhaps they are scoring very well. Another seems unimportant – perhaps an easy par 5, or they are 6 up in the match. Suddenly there is a thought that the shot is very important. Pressure mounts.

The correct way to approach the game is to think rationally, 'I want to do the shot to the best of my ability.' This is a far less pressurised outlook. It shouldn't be a question of busting a gut on one shot and then relaxing on the next. Each should be approached methodically.

An ideal way of understanding the correct mental approach is to play a Texas Scramble. In this you all drive, then you take the best drive, everybody hits from there, and so on. What this does is to teach players not to link shot with shot. There is an element of surprise. It is usually easier to forget one shot and then not think of the next until the choice is made. You learn to separate the shots mentally, seeing one at a time. At the end of the round, the players are usually much less mentally tired than when playing their own ball – simply thinking of the shot facing them when they get there.

NEVER JUDGE THE SHOT UNTIL YOU REACH IT

A golf shot can look very different 10 yards before you reach it from when you finally arrive. The golden rule, again linked to not looking forwards, is never to choose the club until you reach the ball. Don't even contemplate the clubbing until you are there.

DEVELOP A ROUTINE – PRACTICE, PLAY AND PRESSURE

Many golfers spend hours on the practice ground but achieve very little. This is because they are not practising for play, and certainly not for pressure. Many golfers do one thing on the practice ground, then change their technique on the course and finally change it again when it really matters.

Typically it is the approach to shots that changes. The player stands on the practice ground, hitting ball after ball. He looks up once, and gives the ball a thump. Almost before it lands, the next ball is pulled forward, addressed and thumped away. Each time there is one quick look. The address position is probably grooved on target and the shots flow quickly and easily.

See that same player on the course and he probably does something quite different. He now does a little rehearsal. From there he walks round behind the ball, lines up over a spot, addresses the ball and then looks up once, twice and after a little pause, hits it. Quite different from the practice ground. If this is his approach on the course, then this should be the method used on the practice ground. Each shot should be lined up in precisely the same way, holding the balance until the ball lands and watching it to the very finish of its roll.

But then we come to the third situation – pressure. Everything in building up a good golfing method must aim towards its standing up to deterioration under pressure and with tiredness. The likely change now usually involves unnecessary slowing down and trying too hard. Instead of hitting every shot to the best of his ability and leaving it at that, the player probably tries to force the shot. Now he sees the shot as vital, has a couple of practice swings, hitches up the glove, the trousers, fiddles with the clubhead, isn't satisfied with its cleanliness. He then moves behind the ball to choose a spot and can't seem to find one. Eventually, the decision having been made, he moves round to address. He then looks up once, twice, three times. Each time he wears a more pained and worried expression than the time before. Eventually, after much pondering and far more shuffling and deep thought than normal, he seems ready to make a strike. There is silence and stillness. The tension is all too apparent. He then distrusts the club he has chosen and walks away to start all over again!

Practice should rehearse precisely what will happen on the course. Does the player do a waggle or not? Does he look up once, twice or three times? It should be identical in every case – a real routine that withstands pressure. Tom Watson is a model of this. Whether at a pro-am, on the practice ground or on the last tee of a major championship, every movement is precisely the same, never slowing down the preparation or creating tension in a pressure situation.

TWO-SPEED THINKING

The human brain uses two very different decision-making processes. One kind is the emergency type of thinking that gets us out of scrapes. We use it in moving ball games to make quick decisions. Our brain takes in the situation quickly and makes a high-speed, reflex thought and movement. The other kind of decision making is far slower and more thorough. Perhaps you choose between one item and another. You take time to contemplate, weighing things up methodically.

In moving ball games high-speed thinking is used all the time. In a stationary ball game, the danger is of moving from one thought process to another. If you start over- analysing otherwise simple movements they become difficult. This is where we often see the difference in a player from practice to play and pressure. Particularly with the short game, one long firm look with a pitch shot may tell your brain all it needs to know. You assess the situation quickly and thoroughly and rely on instinct and muscle memory to hit the ball on target. In play an added look may be taken, and under pressure, two more. These simply distort the thought process, change it into the slower, more contemplative mode, and with it, feel and coordination are lost. The tendency is to put the error down to lack of concentration and to try even harder on the next occasion. The real remedy is often to rely on the high speed, accurate thought process, if it is this that bears fruit in practice. Some parts of the game require one process, others another. The key is consistency.

PRACTISING FOR PRESSURE

Many golfers change their approach to shots from practice ground to general play and play under pressure. Frequently their method looks brilliant on the practice ground and in a friendly game but in a tournament is slightly lacking. The answer is to put yourself under pressure when you practise. For example, when driving there is no point simply hitting one ball after another with very little aim. Instead, let's assume 14 drives make up a round of golf (ignoring our par 3s), and test yourself until you really can produce 14 perfect drives in succession. Put down targets at the end of the practice ground 20 yards apart and work with each ball as though it mattered. There is no point hitting a less than perfect shot and then thinking, 'I wouldn't do it on the course.' If you do it on the practice ground you are even *more* likely to do it on the course.

The sad thing for the good golfer is that improvement is all about making the bad shots better. Any good golfer can hit perfect shots. Progress means stamping out the bad ones, first of all in practice, then in play and then when it really matters. It is often worth practising drives by teeing up the ball in very slightly different positions, not simply working from the same tee peg over and over again with your feet virtually in the same footprints. Put the club back in your bag, pick it out afresh, go through your whole routine of setting up for a driver. Tee up the ball, tread down behind it, do your practice swing or whatever you normally do. Make each shot count. The only way of being able to hit a drive positively down the eighteenth hole to win an Open Championship is to have done it over and over again in your mind so often that reality and practice merge together when the situation arises.

SETTING GOALS

In order to improve, first make an honest appraisal of your game. Determine what is the weakest part and what the strongest. List the five physical things that will most improve your game, in other words the type of shots. Try to be specific. Then clarify the five 'head' things to improve – confidence, judging distances and so on. Be truthful, and set yourself a target. Look at your expectations for six months or a year ahead and be clear on how you are going to improve. Very often the real improvement comes, not just from shot-making but from factors far easier to correct. Break them down into small goals. OK, so you want to be a scratch golfer; find aims

John Daly – the swing for power – and perfect where it matters, through impact

and targets to get there. Succeed with each of these and the overall aim starts taking shape. It also gives you a sense of achievement, of creeping up on the ultimate goal. Individually your targets may not seem hard to accomplish, but collectively they begin to spell success. Here are a few suggestions for planning the route to stardom.

1 I will prepare the course and have no uncertainties as to distances.
2 I will prepare my equipment well, keep it dry, and clean, and have a couple of spare gloves broken in for a shot or two on the practice range.
3 I will choose the correct club on every shot, and trust the yardage chart and the club chosen.
4 I will look like a winner to everyone watching me – whether winning or losing.
5 I will keep my mind firmly in the present and play every shot to the best of my ability.
6 I will make good, clear decisions, choosing a proper target on every shot.
7 I will attack the golf course and pass the flag whenever I can and the situation allows.
8 I will not search for excuses.
9 I will not be angry with myself or show any anger or frustration.

Then evaluate your performance on your thinking.

As for scoring, again break it down. You want to break 70 for the first time, perhaps. Don't look for the ultimate score. Set out on every round you play to make five birdies. If just off the green at the first, this is a chip for a birdie, not trying to get down in two to save par. Attack the course, one hole after another, until you learn to make more birdies. Play Texas Scrambles to build up your confidence. See just how easily you can get a ball round the

course in 60 or so. You just have to do it without the others helping! But it teaches an attacking form of play. You think of holing chips, short pitches and long putts and soon realise that the ones that miss are closer than normal. If you can count off those five birdies, round after round, scratch golf – or better – soon becomes very possible. If you are already scratch, aim at birdieing six or seven. Come out fighting from the first tee.

If greater distance is the aim, be realistic. Everyone wants to hit the ball further – John Daly, Laura Davies, Davis Love – but don't try for another 30 yards and lose your rhythm. Can you hit the ball not 30 yards but 6 inches further than you have ever hit it before? The answer is probably yes. Then squeeze out another 6 inches today and tomorrow and the next day. Sixty rounds or practice sessions later and those 6 inches build into 10 yards. Ideally mark it off on the range, increasing the distance little by little.

RELAXATION AND TRYING TOO HARD

Golf is not a game where most people do their best when they try their hardest. It is a game most people play best when feeling as relaxed as possible. Tension in the shoulders, arms and hands is usually detrimental to performance.

For most golfers it is better to tackle the most important of events by thinking of them as 'just another round'. How many golfers play their best while doing a few holes walking the dog? The dog is probably far from critical, and the mind relaxed. A friendly round with a few pals is the situation best suited to most people's games. The reason is that there is someone to relax with, someone to talk to. You tend to hit the ball, forget it, carry on a conversation. You get to the next ball, switch off from the conversation and onto the shot. It tends to stop you from thinking from one shot to the next and making judgements too soon.

In a competition situation, however, it is easy for the game to be played in silence. Each player wants to do his best. Perhaps you are faced with someone you have never met before. After the round you sincerely hope you never meet him again. And yet there is nothing wrong with either of you! With no conversation you both start thinking forwards, worrying about the shot ahead, thinking of past errors and trying too hard to make a score. The game gets slower and slower – the players in front usually falling into the same trap. The good shots are stifled by trying too hard.

There are two ways of concentrating on the course. The first is to wrap yourself in a cocoon of concentration on the first tee, trying not to let any extraneous thoughts permeate the outer shell. The second is to learn to switch onto the shot and to switch off between shots. This is how most golfers play their best. Trying to concentrate too hard tends to create tension. A round of golf (at modest speed) is longer than any school exam. The brain is usually exhausted after two or three hours and the game deteriorates. Feeding both mind and body with some food and drink helps mental stamina, but even so the round tends to be exhausting.

The key is to be able to relax and then pinpoint concentration when you arrive at the ball. To relax, if you find this difficult, imagine that tension is a liquid inside the body. Take a few deep breaths and hang the arms down. Imagine the tension, a warm pink fluid, literally dripping into little pools beneath your hands.

To focus your attention and cast aside any unwanted thoughts of the previous conversation, make a statement to yourself. 'Here I am, 150 yards from the target. That is a 7-iron. I want to hit it to the best of my ability.' Switch on, focus on the ball and the target. Hit it, forget it, walk.

CONFIDENCE – FIGHTING FEAR

Golf is a game more punishing than most. In most ball games you can get hurt – a broken nose, ripped-off ears, twisted limbs. In golf, all you risk is a shattered ego. But to many, this is more punishing than physical dangers. Many top class games players, confidently risking life and limb every time they walk on a pitch, are far more frightened of golf and the golf ball. We can make such asses of ourselves. It doesn't matter how great a golfer you are, stupid little errors are round the corner: the short missed putt, the fluffed pitch, the bunker shot catching the face in front. For this reason, you rarely if ever find a conceited golfer – except among those still inexperienced at the nastiness of the game!

In order to play well, it is essential to remove all fear from yourself. In truth, the worst disaster you can face on the golf course is to lose a ball, which costs you money (although in practice you usually find another anyway). And yet many golfers are terrified of making a fool of themselves. The novice seems to think there are eyes staring out of every bush, other golfers always there, chuckling at their errors. In fact, the experienced golfer always turns away and pretends he hasn't seen, only too thankful

that the error wasn't his.

The good golfer is usually concerned over the score. Many are frightened of the card and pencil from the very first tee. One bad hole brings out thoughts of a bad overall score. What will everyone say? Worries over the final total bring out the worst in his game. His mind races ahead, irrationally thinking of the embarrassment facing him. The end of the round will be reached. The marker will want to check the score, calling it out hole by hole and bringing it all back. And then the card will be handed over. A signature will be required, as if to acknowledge all the errors. 'Yes, it was me. I did it. I confess.' From there the wretched score is posted on the board for all to see. And perhaps it will make the newspapers and they will all know. You imagine that everyone will home in on your bad score and think the worse of you, but of course they don't – certainly not those who understand the game.

You have to learn to play the game without fear of failing. You have to ooze confidence, combined with just the right degree of humility.

Consider your own feelings on the course. Rate your confidence, or lack of it, on a scale from 1 to 9. At the lower end – 1 – is a feeling of 'I feel absolutely terrified and wish I wasn't here'. We then work through degrees of being terrified, worried, apprehensive, calm, reasonably confident, positive, very confident and aggressively positive. For many, their rating will always hover around 3 or 4. The good golfer, in any situation, needs to feel at 8 or 9 whether on the first tee, the eighteenth green, or putting to save the match. The aspiring champion needs to feel like a winner and walk like a winner. To those on an adjoining fairway he should portray cool confidence and look as though he is both enjoying the game and succeeding. If faced with a daunting shot, ask yourself how Ernie Els would feel. 'I am Ernie Els. I will hit the ball like Ernie Els.' He isn't going to be worried about losing a new ball.

On the first tee, feel in command of the match even before you tee off. Don't trudge onto the tee nervously and apologetically with the suggestion that you are overawed and honoured to play with your opponent (unless he really is a superstar). Don't utter some drivel about hoping you give him a game. Be confident. 'Hi, I'm George. Have a good game. I'm playing a Titleist 2.' Establish who's boss from the start. Look organised and determined.

LEARN TO PLAY BADLY – AND LOVE IT

Anyone can cope with playing well. The art is to learn to cope with playing badly. If you can still survive and enjoy the game after a horrendous day, you suddenly find they aren't so likely to happen. If you panic, bad turns to worse. Obviously to be a champion you have to have pride in yourself. You want to do your best; you can't be complacent. But fear of bad scores is, in the main, just what causes them. So how do we cope with a bad round?

One player will come in full of smiles. To shouted questions as to how had he done, his first comment is that it was awful, truly awful – a disaster. 'But what was the score?'

'I'm not telling you. It was dreadful, but I enjoyed it. I saw parts of the course I have never seen before, had so much bunker practice my bunker shots feel rejuvenated, and really I feel I have got rid of all the bad shots for the year today. So watch out next month! My score? 94 – no, not 94 gross, 94 nett. But it was fun.'

'Oh, shut up and come and have a beer.'

And then, when others ask after his score, he finds his friends becoming protective (thankful, of course, that it wasn't them). 'He didn't have a good day, but he enjoyed it.' They are all so kind, so sympathetic – at least, any you can call true golfers, with their own ghastly experiences behind them. It wasn't so bad after all. They all come out with their own horror stories of bad rounds and missed putts and the 94 pales into insignificance. A bad round need never hold fears again.

But then there's the other character. He finishes his round, refuses to check the score accurately, scowls at his playing partner, muttering, 'I'd rather tear it up, but put it in if you must', while thrusting the scorecard into his hand. He then storms to the car park, prises open the boot of the car, flings in the clubs, trolley and all still attached, lurches into the driver's seat – still clad in golf shoes – and drives off with a screech of burning rubber. All eyes turn from the clubhouse window. After mumblings and murmurings, everyone knows his score. Blow by blow his round is recounted by the playing partner, exaggerating his every disaster amid squeals of delighted laughter. 'We won't see him here again for a few weeks!'

When the poor soul does finally pluck up courage to attack the course again, his entry into every part of the clubhouse is met with a deathly, embarrassed silence and knowing looks. His next round gets worse, and the one after that worse still, as he remembers the pain from his past experience.

Golf is a game where there are no excuses. Try not to make any – the bad back, the noisy green-keeper, the badly cut hole. Golf, you see, is the only game in which you have your own ball. No one else touches it or influences it. You tee it up, you hit it, you pick it out of the hole, clean it, drop it. Everything that happens to it is your fault and your responsibility. It doesn't matter how well you learn to play, disaster can lurk just round the corner. The trick is to overcome each mishap and accept that golf is a game made up of missed shots. You can wait a lifetime for a hole in one. Every other shot is a miss! Any fool can hit good shots. Real improvement comes from learning to make the bad shots better.

KEYS TO BETTER GOLF

1 *The easiest route to improvement is to learn to do your best swing more often.*

Remember that for many good golfers, improvement is not a question of changing their technique but simply of learning to do their best swing every time. If you can do your best swing 98 per cent instead of 68 per cent of the time, your game will improve. World-class players often have slightly unusual swings but believe in them and repeat them.

2 *Changing your best swing may be harder and may be unnecessary.*

Before making a swing change decide whether it is really necessary and is going to help. Is your real route to success perfecting what you already do, and is a swing change necessarily a swing improvement?

Remember that perfect swingers don't always win, and winners don't often have perfect swings!

3 *Understand your best swing type and perfect it.*

There are many ways of swinging a golf club, all of which are perfect swings. Decide what style of swing you relate to. Compare your own swing with that of one of the great players, find one you feel you can associate with, learn about that type of swing and perfect it. Think long and hard before changing your type of swing.

The backswing may feel like this ...

... but look like this

4 *What we do and what we feel we do can be totally different.*

Remember that the feeling may be of a very dramatic swing change whereas in fact the alteration is minute. The danger is that you lose the feeling of your good swing and yet in reality have made no change at all.

5 *The backswing is simply preparation for the delivery.*

Thinking of the delivery will often correct the backswing. The work of the backswing should be done at address and in the start of the takeaway. If you think of the backswing it sets your brain in the wrong direction.

6 *The most important part of the swing is the impact zone.*

It is also very often the most ignored part. It all happens very quickly and even high-speed cameras can't always unravel precisely what is happening. But the key to good golf is to be perfect through impact.

7 *Altering the follow-through often corrects the delivery pattern and allows the easiest changes.*

Remember that the follow-through is not simply the result of a good swing. If you think of a 'position' in the follow-through it will often steer you into doing the right movements in the backswing and through the delivery. The follow-through also gives you feedback and can be the easiest part of the swing to correct and often the most effective.

8 *The swing needs to be as simple as possible; the game is hard enough.*

Remember that the golf swing takes only a couple of seconds. We can only pinpoint two or three swing thoughts at the most. The swing should become as automatic as possible to allow the brain time and energy to concentrate on ball control and scoring.

9 *Whenever you find the perfect feel – **practise** – and try to keep it as long as possible.*

The perfect golf swing is often rather like a dream. You try and remember it, but the feeling disappears before you can get hold of it!

10 *Work at clubface control.*

Remember that the whole idea of the swing is to deliver the clubface correctly to the ball. The tiniest inaccuracies of the clubface striking the ball can produce imperfect shots. Work at feel as the clubface strikes the ball and learn perfect feel of clubface on ball with every club from wedge to driver. Don't let there be any club in the bag that you don't like. Don't practise only with your best friends; concentrate on making friends with the clubs you like least.

SO YOU WANT TO BE A WINNER

Learning to win at golf is a strange mixture of technique and mental strength. It is a combination of *swing, shot-making and scoring*. The first, without the second and third, rarely if ever wins. The second and third, with a consistent, even if imperfect technique, are often highly successful.

See the ability to score as an art all of its own. Enter every tournament you play with realistic expectations. If there are 50 other competitors it takes a lot to finish ahead of them. Don't pressurise yourself. You arrive at the tournament without having won it. If you go home without having won it, what changes? Only a major championship or winning huge sums of money changes your life. The monthly medal that causes such anguish one day is probably forgotten by the following week. See the game in context. It is never an ego trip, even for the best. When you sign your name to the scorecard be content and always see something good in every round you play. Learn from your mistakes and never stop learning and developing in every facet of this marvellous, but complicated, game.

11 TEN PERFECT SWINGS

SWING TYPES

One of the dangers of reading about golf swings is that the writer – usually a tournament player – has a specific type of swing and may not know, or indeed may not want to know, how other types of swings feel. The error indeed, for a method type teacher is that he or she is locked too closely into one type of swing concept, trying to mould every player into that same pattern. It is dangerous.

I was discussing one particular highly thought of teacher with one of his ever faithful disciples who expressed the very great merits of the method – or so he thought – in that whether he (a superstar) or a middle aged lady beginner went for help, the maestro's methods would be the same. Standardisation! But, of course, it is a fallacy. The fool, and he would be one, who tried to turn a Lee Trevino into a Jack Nicklaus, or a Greg Norman into a Bernhard Langer – or vice versa in either case, would do no one a favour. Each has a perfect swing of its type. Each type has its potential flaws.

Is there a perfect swing? I suppose in reality Ian Woosnam's at its best is the simplest. Watch it, whack it, wait for the applause. But if you are 6 foot 4 inches instead of 5 foot 4 inches the concepts are different. The feeling for the very tall golfer is like Ian standing on a very unpleasant sidehill lie a foot above the ball. Suddenly not so simple.

Then of course some are right handed, others left. Some naturally are cutters – faders of a golf ball just as they would be a cutter in any racquet game. Others are drawers, hookers, topspinners with a racquet. The natural shape and swing type is often there from the word 'go'.

I believe it is difficult and dangerous to change swing types and dangerous for the coach of top class players to be inflexible, trying to standardise and steer all towards one type. To teach well at a top class level one needs a flexible approach, being prepared to see where the pupil fits into the swing spectrum and to create an understanding of technical intricacies applicable to him.

If the player identifies with Mark James or Lee Trevino, so must you. It is no good homing in on the fact that the club shaft doesn't point 'on target' at the top of the backswing. Nor can we take a player in the Paul Azinger mould with a grip which in most would produce a chronic hook and work at folding away the left arm or increased hand action. At a certain stage where we see a player with two 'wrongs' compensating and making a right, we have to leave well alone. Work at repetition and if necessary the most gradual and most delicate piece of fine tuning to modify the two weaknesses hand in hand.

So let's have a look at swing types. There are perhaps ten perfect styles of swing we can identify. It is a question of relating to one or other of these, learning the good points and bad points of each and then working at perfecting that type of swing without trying to cross from one to the other without very careful thought.

SIMPLICITY – IAN WOOSNAM

This is perhaps the golf swing in its simplest form. Easy for a small player to achieve; difficult for the tall player. Ian's height makes it unnecessary to show much flex in the legs or bend from the hips. The swing is just a coordinated turn to the right and turn to the left with the arms moving back and through, and naturally up and down, in sympathy with the turn.

Swing concepts – probably emphasis on the left arm in the backswing, ensuring a tightish turn instead of a loose one. Perfect balance is essential to cope with the speed of the swing and force of the hit. The plane of the swing follows the club all the way. The club shaft angle at address is seen in the left arm at the top of the backswing and again with the club shaft in the follow-through.

Potential problems for this style of player are often that, because the swing seems so easy, it becomes casual and a bit sloppy – a danger of not watching the ball long enough.

The swing seems so easy you can't imagine why everyone else doesn't do the same!

Ian Woosnam – watch it, whack it and wait for the applause!

GREG NORMAN – A MODEL FOR THE TALL PLAYER

The problems for players the height of Greg Norman, Nick Faldo and Ernie Els are enormous. For us, it would be like having to play from a continuous sidehill lie, standing many inches above the ball. Balance is more difficult, and the plane of the swing becomes too upright. It is then difficult to attack the ball from the inside, the left leg gets in the way and there is often a feeling of insufficient space.

The tall golfer most easily falls into the trap of adopting a high and wide swing (like Jack Nicklaus's) with its potential flaws – the ball too far forward, left leg bowing out and the plane of arms and shoulders steeper than one would want.

Greg found great success as a 'high and wide' swinger, but with the ever-present potential problem of the hips tipping through impact, the right shoulder working under the ball blocking away to the right. It happened under pressure and cost him several major victories. The swing is now much flatter and on plane, the clubshaft at address dictating the plane of the whole swing. He displays excellent posture, gets the club well behind himself into a wrist position where he can deliver power from the inside, clears his left leg through well (with the slight idiosyncrasy of a sliding left foot) and is able to stay on plane. Good posture, a tight turn and tall, level clearance are the keys to this type of swing.

The Greg Norman of old, high and wide with tilting hips and shoulders

Greg Norman showing
the perfect posture and
plane for a tall golfer

SIMPLICITY – TURN AND LIFT – TOM WATSON

Here the body turns very naturally to right and left but with a more definite lift of the arms. Instead of just 'turn – turn', it becomes more 'turn and lift – turn and lift'. There is a distinct separation between arms and body. The body goes round and round and the arms go up, down, up. This style of player needs very often to ensure that the hips clear in the follow-through as the arms come up and over. The two separate. The hips go round in the finish and the arms go up. The club shaft is now going to be more down the back, i.e. nearer the vertical than at address. The concept here is definitely one of separation. The shoulders turn fairly horizontally in the back-swing and the arms lift into a fairly high position; then in the throughswing the hips clear while the arms lift. The 'separation' feeling is often needed for players prone to hooking. Too much togeth-erness can allow the clubface to close. Hips through, arms up often protects the left side of the course. It is a swing which is often good for those with a tendency to hook, particularly through a tendency to be flat through and beyond impact. It gives the feeling of working away from the left of the course, spinning the hips and lifting the arms being the very opposite of the action of the natural drawer. The clubhead moves through 'toe up' in the throughswing to produce the high finish, and with it sees the club-face work through square or a touch open. The arms fold *up*, with little feeling of extension and width, clubhead moving up towards the target beyond impact. The one drawback is perhaps an overly quick hip turn through, resulting, if it hap-pens, in more cut than the player might require.

Again, this is an extremely simple swing, just two movements – turning the body to the right and lifting the arms, turning the body to the left and lifting the arms. So simple that you might imagine the game is totally straight-forward!

Tom Watson, shoulders
turning almost horizontally,
arms lifting for one of the
simplest swings in golf

UP-AND-OVER – THE FLAT SWINGERS – MARK JAMES OR LEE TREVINO

The flat swinger often pulls the left arm and shoulder up in the takeaway, right elbow in, left arm across. The shoulder turn is minimal and the back of the left hand is flat, wrists cocked back rather than up. The swing will not point in the direction of the shot but is laid off left of it. (If the swing went a lot further it would eventually get round there, but it doesn't and shouldn't.) The player has the club very much behind him and will always attack the ball from well inside, right hand generating power from behind. The right hand is in a position where it can hit. Incidentally the inside attack will always be relative to the line of feet – not necessarily the shot. The inside attack of the flat swing is often prone to pushing, hence in Trevino's case the feet are aimed left to enable the ball to start on target.

The flat swing of this kind is not produced from a flat takeaway but from the reverse. The swing is much more one of lift and turn rather than

Mark James and Lee Trevino – the drawer and the fader. Mark James' action shows the arms closing onto each other, left elbow down and in for a draw. Lee Trevino shows the left elbow pulling away, arms spreading, for a fade.

turn and lift, flattening the left arm and back of the hand over. The perfect swing of this type can be tremendously effective. Most players would find it impossible to do – shouldn't try if it doesn't feel natural. The left shoulder is very visible to the player in the backswing, so the attack probably feels alarmingly shallow to anyone to whom this is not natural.

The drawback for this type of player is often the inability to get a high, floating ball when the need arises. It is also a swing which tends to be asymmetrical. It doesn't perhaps look anything like as attractive as a Payne Stewart, but the flat swing with a shallow, inside attack can be extremely effective. Once the club is returned to the ball the player often blocks with the hips and legs, perhaps reducing the likelihood of a truly consistent swing. The ball position can be crucial, but it is a swing with many merits.

Mark James allows the club to turn over through and beyond impact, moving the ball right to left. Trevino holds the back of the left wrist very firm for a blocked fade, right forearm never crossing the left. Not the most attractive of swings but perfect in their own way, and effective!

THE HANDS AND WRISTS SWINGER –
FRED COUPLES

The methods of most tournament professionals involve little or no sensation of hand action. To most, the wrists probably feel fairly passive. Many professionals say they have no feeling of using the hands, and try, indeed, to eliminate hand action and use a swing that feels to be body and arms. Other golfers feel the swing to be controlled from the hands and wrists – and with this produce the flowing action of a Bobby Jones, Fred Couples or Payne Stewart. Now, instead of a concept of a tightly wound, coiled turn, the feeling may be of a relatively loose turn, definitely cocking the left wrist upwards and supporting the club on the left thumb. From here it is all about timing the down and throughswing. A full, free turn of the hips back and through, the clubhead whipping the ball away with a release of the wrists. Perhaps now considered to be slightly old-fashioned, this swing relies on hand action and feeling in the hands to return the clubface squarely every time. It was a style of swing that was more common with the small, British size, 1.62 inch ball which required a feeling for hand action to tweak the ball up into the air. The emphasis on hands and wrists produces a cupping of the left wrist in the backswing and allows the clubface to appear to move from open to closed through impact rather rapidly, with a little more susceptibility to directional errors. Fred shows a very marked action of moving from a cupped position at the top of the backswing by dropping and setting the club behind him to return on a shallower, more inside path than is suggested by the backswing.

For the player who is a swinger, timing is crucial. The movement through of the body and the swinging down of the arms coordinate perfectly. If the body leads, a fade or slice is likely. If legs or body lag, the clubhead may lead with a tendency to close. This kind of player often needs a very definite sensation of 'waiting for it' at the top of the backswing (very obvious in Fred's swing), ensuring that the body stays turned away long enough to get the arms and club down on the inside.

Certainly the most elegant type of swings, giving the impression of relaxation and timing but perhaps prone to being just a touch loose and with a little less control of the clubface; very dependent on timing and on rhythm rather tremendous fitness and speed. Hand-eye coordination is vital. The ball goes on-target because of feel, visualising the target and instinctively propelling it there rather than through a precise method.

Fred Couples – relaxation and timing

THE DRAWERS – TOM LEHMAN AND SANDY LYLE

Tom Lehman probably typifies the perfect action for the drawer. The ball consistently starts slightly right of target and bends back in. The action is not one of wrist roll or closing the face but of addressing the ball a touch towards the toe and moving the clubface in-to-out across the ball to impart spin. The left wrist is firm and flat at the top of the backswing and the wrists remain firm through impact as spin is imparted.

Hand in hand with this goes an action of starting the ball out to the right to bring it back in. The legs and hips stay turned away at the top of the backswing to give the swing time to return from the inside. Leg action in the throughswing is fairly minimal and late, with restricted hip clearance in the followthrough. At the end of the swing the hips and right knee still face away slightly to the right of target with the right foot being pulled on through but giving the appearance of being slightly restricted. The slow hip and leg release is a sure sign of a player whose play is dominated by working the ball right to left. Sandy Lyle shows much the same action, legs lagging, hip clearance slow.

The danger here is of the legs failing to clear and the arms being forced into a scissor-type action beyond impact, clubface closing. With this action the real problem is almost certainly a hook if the legs block. In reality the player perhaps doesn't hook but instead blocks and pushes shots to the right. Players who draw the ball in this way are often afraid of shots with trouble just left of the green or fairway. The feeling then needs to be of opening up the hips in the throughswing, ensuring the leg action doesn't become too slow, and resisting the feeling of standing closed and allowing for an ever greater draw (or hook). This swing is often seen with strong players of a large build who use minimal leg action, and as a result they start working the ball right to left to bring it back from the right.

Tom Lehman – a perfect example of a 'drawer', firm wrists and an in-to-out action, legs almost inactive through impact

Sandy Lyle – moving the ball right to left, with slow leg action, clubface working in-to-out across the ball

THE CUTTERS – COLIN MONTGOMERIE AND BRUCE LIETZKE

The action of the cutter (some would say slicer) is typified by Colin Montgomerie and Bruce Lietzke, i.e. players who start the ball many yards left of target and allow it to cut back in, often with a very pronounced bend. Colin's swing shows a marked sway of the hips, perhaps coming about through a low head position at address and bottom in rather than bottom out posture. From here the hip slide takes the club up and away on the outside with a relatively steep out-to-in attack and very active hips through impact. The disadvantage for most golfers in cutting the ball to this extent is loss of distance. With both Lietzke and Montgomerie length is no handicap. The great advantage of slicing the ball in this way is that it can be started down the left side of the hole with a very consistent shape, plenty of width of fairway to play with and a soft landing impact. It is very safe. It does, however, require good timing for a professional. Any speeding up of the hands through impact is likely to result in a shot pulled left, with unwanted extra length.

Colin Montgomerie aiming left and cutting it back in with a very active hip action

Colin Montgomerie and
Bruce Lietzke showing the
very active hip and leg
action of the typical fader or
slicer

HIGH AND WIDE – JACK NICKLAUS

For those learning golf in the 1960s, Jack Nicklaus had a technique which was at that time seen as an oddity. Instead of the conventional classic swing of turning, working at roundness, an inside takeaway and inside attack, here was Jack taking the club back straight, wide and high with a flying right elbow.

As Jack became the undisputed best player in the world, so these actions came to be copied – and indeed a generation of high and wide swingers emerged. The club moved in a straighter path back and through, the ball was played further forward and the hips and left leg no longer cleared in quite the same way. It became acceptable to finish with a bowed left leg – a definite no-no before 1970 or so for anyone of ordinary height. Many with a more classical rounded swing found it impossible to reconcile a fairly straight back and a through swing with a square clubface toe-up (or nearly toe-up) at hip-height both back and through. Many found that the straight back and through approach could be employed only by moving the clubface from slightly more shut to open. There were those who talked of curling under with the left wrist in the backswing and holding the clubface up beyond impact. In truth the swing is off its plane, but it unquestionably works for those who see the swing that way. To some teachers it is totally wrong, but for some players it is totally right.

Players like Nick Faldo and Greg Norman started their professional careers in the same mould as Nicklaus. With this swing they both developed tendencies to tip and tilt the hips and work under in the through-swing. Both have since moved away from this action to greater success, but there are many for whom the Nicklaus action of a low head position, steep shoulder plane and high arm action is the way to play.

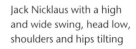

Jack Nicklaus with a high
and wide swing, head low,
shoulders and hips tilting

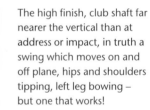

The high finish, club shaft far
nearer the vertical than at
address or impact, in truth a
swing which moves on and
off plane, hips and shoulders
tipping, left leg bowing –
but one that works!

If you identify with the Jack Nicklaus type of swing, remember that attacking the ball from the inside becomes increasingly difficult. Nicklaus did; most don't. Remember too that while the club swings up and down rather than round behind the player, the wrist-cock also works in an up-and-down direction. The right hand cannot release or the whole action tends to become right-side dominant. Players with this type of swing often have to work at attacking the ball from the inside by dropping right hip and shoulder down behind it, hence the bowing out of the left leg (also a result of having the ball well forward). The swing does not perhaps stand up as well as others in advancing years, the bowing out of the left leg and the constant twisting appearing to cause back problems.

ABOVE AND RIGHT: Nicklaus at full stretch at the peak of his career

TOGETHERNESS – BERNHARD LANGER

If Jack Nicklaus typifies the high and wide swing and Tom Watson the separation of hips through and arms up, Bernhard Langer displays the opposite, a flat but symmetrical swing. The planes of both backswing and throughswing match totally. In theory the strong left-hand grip of Langer looks as though he would hook, but in reality the right hand and clubface are lined up to produce clubface control. If anything the left hand being so strong probably produces a rather dominant left arm at impact which wants to block through impact leaving the face open. This is not necessarily the case in Bernhard's swing but is common in those who copy it.

Bernhard's flat roll away, collapse away followthrough, arms rolling on to each other and staying close, works the clubface through squarely. It is a swing where the back of the left hand starts uppermost and wants to come through uppermost, with the left thumb behind the shaft through delivery. In some this grip position produces the 'please do not let me hook' swing of Arnold Palmer and Paul Azinger. Left to itself you feel the clubface would close into a monumental hook, resulting in a player blocking with the left arm, left elbow out through impact and 'holding it off' for a straight shot or fade.

Bernhard grips as though he is going to hook and plays a beautiful soft draw. The point about this swing is that the arms fold away and onto each other in the followthrough. The left elbow folds inwards, never outwards, in the finish. Players believing they copy this usually allow the left elbow to spread, holding the face open. This swing type is very rarely seen but is certainly very effective. In essence the left hand is in a strong position which the theory books tell us would hook but in practice will more likely produce a push. The right-hand position is perfect and the swing is on plane all the way, backswing and throughswing matching totally. With Bernhard, as with other players in this mould, there are times when the feeling is one of having to fight a hook. In this instance the followthrough needs to have a feeling of height, of holding back with the right arm and hand and allowing the left elbow to spread with a feeling of blocking out the hook.

Bernhard Langer with a flattish, tight swing

THE RIGHT SIDED SWING – NICK FALDO – THE TECHNICIAN

David Leadbetter has done for the tall player what needed doing – teaching them to swing with the plane of a man of 5 foot 8 inches. The tall golfer often faces the problems most of us encounter when standing several inches above the ball, with a tendency to work under with hips and shoulders. Nick's efforts have largely been to produce a flatter plane of swing to eliminate a tipping and tilting of the hips. It is an action dominated by the right side, turning the whole body away against the resistance of the legs and then allowing the right side to hit but with the right hand and wrist held back through impact. If anything the problem comes if the plane of the followthrough becomes flatter than that of the backswing, the two halves not quite matching, with a dominant right shoulder producing the occasional dragged shot to the left.

Just as Nicklaus produced by his example a generation of high and wide swingers, so Faldo is in danger of leading a generation of golfers to overly flat finishes. In the Faldo finish, as in the Langer one, there is no question of the arms separating. They stay very much together – left elbow in and under. The more in and under, the more likely a draw; the more out

and up with the left elbow, the greater the chance for cut. Those who copy often forget this and produce elbow spread at the end – the very antithesis of the Faldo (or Langer) methods. Swing concepts for those who identify with Faldo – for height, build and dedication to work on complex techniques – are superb posture, getting the wrists hingeing backwards rather than up, from there turning the shoulders fully on a flat enough plane, coiling against the resistance of the legs, moving the left leg away in the downswing, hitting with the right side in control, right wrist still hinged, togetherness in the finish and lots, lots more! For the tall player, Nick Faldo demonstrates the concept of a constant posture through the swing. He starts at address with a specific hip bend and returns to address with that same posture. The top half then works on through in the finish, right shoulder riding very high rather than arching under. As a result the head moves several inches to the right and left during the swing. The typical action for the tall player is often more one where the head stays still and the body twists and turns under, or where there is a release and lift beyond impact.

A complex swing, requiring a mechanical approach and constant fine-tuning to harness the right side and keep it in check. It should be seen in the context of a tall man fighting against an over-upright plane.

Nick Faldo – complex swing thoughts but a model for the tall golfer

THE MAJESTIC FINISH – SEVE BALLESTEROS

Lastly, For those who identify with Seve, take it back low, finish high and simply feel the clubface with your hands and heart to magic the ball whichever way the mood takes you. This approach depends on flair and inevitably has a little too much variation from hole to hole and week to week when things are not going 100 per cent. This is a swing which even Seve finds hard to reproduce daily. The concepts for this type of player are clubface feel and preferably a stationary, totally repetitive finish.

Seve in fact takes the club fairly straight back in the takeaway, loops slightly inside in the downswing so that he attacks the ball from the inside, moves into impact and then stands up. In other words, his head is several inches higher in the follow-through than at address. The feeling is very much one of instinctive clubface control, not with forearm control and a lot of hand and wrist action. A marvellous swing but one that depends on perfect feel rather than truly repeatable mechanics.

Seve is another player who has changed the plane of his swing. His swing until early 1994 was unquestionably off its plane. His posture would get lower and more 'squatty' under pressure,

instead of tall and majestic as when at his best. The action was typified by a backswing which was straight back and high, dropping in and under on the downswing. It was hard to reproduce on a daily basis – brilliant one week and horrible (by his standards) the next. The 'new' Seve now sees the swing move on a much flatter plane in the backswing, but from a tall, backside up posture, following perfectly the angle of the clubshaft, with backswing, downswing and throughswing now all matching.

The impression is still one of swinging slightly from low to high, allowing a tall, majestic finish with slightly more height than the backswing, but the need for an inside loop has gone. For those who relate to this type of swing there is always a need to watch the ball long enough through impact before allowing the swing to rise. And, as with Seve himself, there is a need to ensure that the right shoulder doesn't edge up with anxiety momentarily too soon when faced with trouble to the right of the course.

The player who relates to this swing may feel a shallow inside attack with a feeling of extension out and up beyond impact, clubface moving fractionally in-to-out across the ball to impart drawspin, combined with height to the finish and carry to the shots.

Seve Ballesteros showing a perfect posture and plane ...

... and a majestic finish!